KU-036-792

Home Office Research Study 265

Reducing alcohol-related violence and disorder: an evaluation of the 'TASC' project

Mike Maguire and Hilary Nettleton
with the assistance of Andrew Rix and Stephen Raybould

The views expressed in this report are those of the authors, not necessarily those of the Home Office (nor do they reflect Government policy).

Home Office Research, Development and Statistics Directorate
March 2003

Home Office Research Studies

The Home Office Research Studies are reports on research undertaken by or on behalf of the Home Office. They cover the range of subjects for which the Home Secretary has responsibility. Other publications produced by the Research, Development and Statistics Directorate include Findings, Statistical Bulletins and Statistical Papers.

The Research, Development and Statistics Directorate

RDS is part of the Home Office. The Home Office's purpose is to build a safe, just and tolerant society in which the rights and responsibilities of individuals, families and communities are properly balanced and the protection and security of the public are maintained.

RDS is also part of National Statistics (NS). One of the aims of NS is to inform Parliament and the citizen about the state of the nation and provide a window on the work and performance of government, allowing the impact of government policies and actions to be assessed.

Therefore –

Research Development and Statistics Directorate exists to improve policy making, decision taking and practice in support of the Home Office purpose and aims, to provide the public and Parliament with information necessary for informed debate and to publish information for future use.

First published 2003
Application for reproduction should be made to the Communications and Development Unit, Room 201, Home Office, 50 Queen Anne's Gate, London SW1H 9AT.
© Crown copyright 2003   ISBN   1 84082 999 0
ISSN   0072 6435

Foreword

The growth of the night-time economy in many cities has resulted in heightened concern about associated crime and disorder, especially that of alcohol-related violence. The Tackling Alcohol-related Street Crime (TASC) project was a police-led multi-agency scheme aimed at reducing alcohol-related crime and disorder in Cardiff and Cardiff Bay. It involved a range of interventions including dialogue between the police and the licensed trade, measures aimed at improving the quality and behaviour of door staff, targeted policing operations and support for victims of alcohol-related assaults.

The project was associated with an overall decrease in alcohol-related assaults in Cardiff and Cardiff Bay. There were also significant reductions in violence and disorder associated with specific clubs against which targeted policing operations took place. This report describes the project and its main outcomes and highlights key examples of good practice for those seeking to implement similar projects.

Chris Kershaw
Crime and Policing Group
Research, Development and Statistics Directorate

Acknowledgments

The authors would like to thank all members of the TASC project team, and all the partner organisations involved, for generously giving of their time to assist the evaluation, as well as providing a great deal of valuable data. We would also like to thank the following individuals for their help in providing extra information and commenting on early drafts of this report: Professor Roy Light, University of West of England; Professor Jonathon Shepherd, University of Wales College of Medicine; Inspector Tony Rees, South Wales Police; Victoria Swainson, data analyst; and the anonymous reviewers appointed by the Home Office. Finally, special thanks to Fiona McLean and Karen Bullock of the Home Office Crime and Policing Group for their patience and assistance in guiding and facilitating the project.

The Home Office Crime and Policing Group would like to thank Verity Ridgman of the Property and Road Crime Reduction Unit and Tracy Budd of the Drugs and Alcohol Research Unit for their comments on this draft.

The authors

Mike Maguire is Professor of Criminology and Criminal Justice in the School of Social Sciences, Cardiff University.

Hillary Nettleton was formally a Research Associate in the School of Social Sciences, Cardiff University.

Andrew Rix and Stephen Raybould are Research Consultants at CRG, Cardiff.

Contents

Executive summary

The Tackling Alcohol-related Street Crime (TASC) project was a police-led multi-agency scheme launched in July 2000 under the Home Office Targeted Policing Initiative, with the aim of reducing alcohol-related crime and disorder in central Cardiff and Cardiff Bay. Its interventions included:

- focused dialogue between the police and members of the licensed trade, mainly through an active Licensees Forum;
- measures aimed at improving the quality and behaviour of door staff;
- attempts to influence licensing policy and practice;
- measures aimed at publicising the problem of alcohol-related violent crime;
- targeted policing operations directed at crime and disorder 'hot spots';
- a cognitive behavioural programme for repeat offenders ('COV-AID');
- a training programme for bar staff ('Servewise');
- a programme of education about alcohol for school age children; and
- support for victims of alcohol-related assaults attending hospital.

The project created a dedicated database, maintained by the data analyst, which combined information from police sources and the local hospital. This revealed that:

- alcohol related incidents were heavily concentrated on Friday and Saturday nights. Sixty-one per cent involved physical violence, the remainder 'disorder';
- over half (most of them violent) occurred in or just outside licensed premises. Incidents of disorder were more likely to occur elsewhere on the streets;
- most of those involved as offenders or victims were young white males. Forty-two per cent of arrestees had previous arrests for violence or public order offences;
- 'door staff' were involved as victims or alleged assailants in 16 per cent of all violent incidents. Sixty-one were arrested over the 30 month period monitored;
- the most common form of assault was punching or kicking, but at least 10 per cent of cases involved bottles or glasses; the use of knives was rare; and
- most injuries were minor, but 15 per cent of assault victims suffered broken bones and 12 per cent major cuts.

Outcomes

A comparison of the first 12 months after the launch of the project with the previous 12 months indicated an overall decrease of four per cent in incidents involving alcohol-related assaults. This occurred despite a ten per cent increase in licensed premise capacity in central Cardiff. During the same period, incidents of violence against the person rose elsewhere in South Wales. The researchers' best estimate is that, during its first year, the project helped to reduce the expected level of violent incidents by eight per cent: that is, it prevented about 100 assaults. If it is assumed that just one (or more) of these incidents would have involved a serious wounding, cost-effectiveness analysis suggests that the project represented 'value for money'.

By contrast, there was a 49 per cent increase in incidents of alcohol-related disorder. However, this is a much more slippery concept than 'alcohol-related assault', and the figures given are more susceptible to changes in police recording practices. Even if the figures are accepted at face value, two important qualifications should be noted:

1. The rise slowed markedly during the evaluation period: the increases for the first three six-month periods after launch, compared to the equivalent period of the year before, were 75 per cent, 29 per cent and 3 per cent.

2. Virtually all the rise in disorder was accounted for by one street in Cardiff, which had the densest concentration of pubs and clubs and several newly opened premises.

There were significant reductions in violent and disorderly incidents occurring in or just outside individual pubs and clubs which were the subject of carefully targeted policing operations. The most successful of these, lasting eight weeks, was followed by reductions of 41 per cent and 36 per cent in such incidents in and around the two clubs targeted. The reductions were also sustained over time. Operations targeted at whole streets, rather than individual premises, were less successful.

Overall, the TASC project was most successful in terms of its targeted work with individual premises. Its most fruitful partnership arrangements were with the Licensees Forum, through which joint attempts were made to improve security arrangements – including staff training – both generally and in premises where the TASC database indicated that the numbers of incidents were high or rising.

On the other hand, it was less successful in persuading 'key players ' in the County Council, breweries or other relevant companies to adopt broader strategic approaches to the prevention of late night violence and disorder. Its best achievements here were improved registration, training and disciplinary systems for door staff. However, it made little headway in influencing planning policy or in slowing the expansion of licensed premises in 'saturated' areas of Cardiff. It also failed to get general agreement to changes in alcohol marketing strategies. It is argued that, while better management of individual premises is necessary to the reduction of alcohol-related violence and disorder, attention to wider issues arising from the growth of the 'night time economy' is vital to the long term success of crime prevention in this field.

Key examples of 'good practice'

- The creation of effective links with managers of licensed premises, especially through an active Licensees Forum.
- A well resourced project team, including a manager of sufficient rank and experience and an analyst with good access to police data systems, combined with full integration of the project into police objectives and priorities.
- The maintenance of an accurate and up-to-date dedicated database, drawing on both police and hospital sources, used not only to identify emerging problems, but to guide remedial visits to licensed premises.
- The development of standard training, registration and disciplinary systems for door staff in the city.
- Wide promotion of the project's objectives using a range of innovative sources eg bus campaigns, websites and electronic public information display screens.
- Attempts to engage major players in both the public and private sectors in broader dialogue about the strategic management of the 'late night economy'.

1.   Introduction and overview

This report presents an evaluation of the Tackling Alcohol-Related Street Crime (TASC) project, funded under the Targeted Policing Initiative (TPI) within the Home Office Crime Reduction Programme. TASC's principal objective was to reduce the level of alcohol-related violence and disorder in Cardiff city centre and the Cardiff Bay area. Like other TPI projects, it was based on inter-agency partnership and adopted a focused, 'problem solving' approach, seeking innovative solutions to specific forms of offending in specific locations. The lead agency was South Wales Police, and the partners included Cardiff County Council, the University Hospital of Wales and – vitally – the private sector, in the shape of the Cardiff Licensees Forum. Staff were appointed in late 1999, and the project was launched in June 2000. The initial Home Office grant (£500,000) ended in March 2002, but the project received extra funding to continue with reduced staffing for six months as a 'demonstration project'. This evaluation is based on data collected up to December 2001.

When first set up, TASC was among a relatively small number of projects pioneering multi-agency work to reduce this type of offending, but there has since been a rapid expansion of similar schemes in city and town centres across Britain. Indeed, the TASC project team received numerous visits from members of other police forces and local authorities keen to draw upon their experience. As yet, however, little is known about the effectiveness of these schemes – let alone about the effectiveness of variations in approach that have been adopted – in reducing alcohol-related violence and disorder. There has also been a growing debate about the relationship between alcohol-related violence and broader issues such as the growth of a new 'night-time economy' based around expansions in the leisure and entertainment industries and liberalisation of licensing policies (see, for example Hobbs *et al.*, 2000; Lister *et al.*, 2001; LGA, 2002): this raises important questions about the extent to which responsibility for controlling violence and disorder should fall upon individual licensed premises, the police or local authorities. This evaluation, which draws on an unusual and specially constructed database of relevant incidents, provides some useful empirical evidence to inform discussions of all the above issues.

The report is divided into six chapters. This chapter provides an overview of the aims of the project and the context within which it was designed and implemented. Chapter 2 describes the various elements of the project in more detail and presents a 'process evaluation' of its implementation. Chapter 3 draws on the TASC database to provide a statistical account of patterns of violence and disorder in central Cardiff. It also compares the pictures painted by various types of police data and by data from the Accident and Emergency (A & E) Unit of the local hospital – a topical issue as the Home Office is considering the potential of hospital data as an alternative indicator of trends in violence (see, for example, Simmons, 2000). Chapter 4 considers the evidence as to whether, and to what extent, the TASC project had an impact on the incidence of violence and disorder, either at the level of individual 'hot spots' or across the targeted area as a whole. Chapter 5 outlines the costs of the project and offers some conclusions about its cost-effectiveness. Chapter 6 provides a summary and conclusions, as well as some recommendations and lessons on 'good practice'.

Context

The TASC project was conceived and implemented during a period of rapid change in Cardiff, which has grown into a leading centre for the leisure and entertainment industries, and a regular host for major sporting and cultural events. Considerable investment in the city continues to take place as a result of the development of the Millennium Stadium and the regeneration of Cardiff Bay. It is estimated that Cardiff receives annually at least nine million day visitors and two million overnight visitors (Cardiff Research Centre, 2000). In 2002, it is estimated that tourism (in its broadest sense) will contribute over £300 million to the local economy.

A key part of this development – as in many other major cities – has been the growth of a lucrative 'night-time economy'. Over recent years, members of the leisure, entertainment and brewing industries, with the support of the local authority, have consciously set out to attract large numbers of young people into the city centre in the evenings and to keep them there well into the night (especially on Fridays and Saturdays) in order to sell alcohol, fast food and entertainment. This aim has been greatly assisted by national changes in licensing policy and practice. As recommended in the *Good Practice Guide: Licensing* (Justices' Clerks' Society, 1999; see also Light, 2000), the concept of 'need' has been all but discounted by justices' committees in licensing decisions, leaving the number of premises selling alcoholic drinks to be determined primarily by market forces. Importantly, too, special hours licences have become much easier to obtain. The result has been a proliferation of licensed premises in the city centre – especially large 'theme' pubs and clubs – selling alcohol into the early hours of the morning. Evidence collected by *Cardiff Marketing* shows that the city has become a key venue for late-night revellers from right across the South Wales area. Revellers typically begin drinking in the early evening in pubs and then move on to the larger clubs holding extended licences, staying into the early hours of the morning before emerging to look for fast food outlets and taxi ranks.

Such patterns of behaviour inevitably generate a certain amount of crime and disorder, both acquisitive (eg robbery or theft from the person) and expressive (eg violence and 'rowdiness'). The focus of the TASC project was on the latter kinds of incident, in particular on assaults and disorderly behaviour associated with the consumption of alcohol.[1] Such incidents may take place within licensed premises themselves, in confrontations with 'door staff' outside such premises, or in the street (for example, when groups or individuals clash in queues for taxis to return home). They may also, of course, occur on the journey home (eg in assaults on taxi drivers or train or bus staff) and after arrival home (in the form of assaults on partners and children). However, neither domestic violence nor violence on transport were addressed by the TASC project, whose sphere of activity was limited to a small and mainly non-residential area in which the predominant forms of violence and disorder occurred in licensed premises or the streets – namely, two police sectors covering the central shopping and entertainment area of Cardiff (Appendix 1 shows a map of this area), and the regenerated docklands area of Cardiff Bay, which contains several large dance clubs, bars and pubs.

Even limiting the focus in this way, it is obvious that alcohol-related violence and disorder constitute a problem which spans public, semi-public and private space, and hence that any effective attempt to reduce or control it has to involve both the public and private sectors – at the very least, well-trained security staff within (or 'on the doors' of) licensed premises and police officers on the streets. However, the question will also be raised whether even a combination of high quality club management and effective street policing can have a significant and lasting effect without parallel attention to broader issues such as city planning, licensing and transport policies, and the marketing strategies of major leisure organisations and breweries – issues which require the co-operation and serious involvement of both local authorities and major commercial players. As will be described in the report, the TASC project was driven initially by traditional, relatively narrowly focussed 'situational crime prevention' and 'targeted policing' approaches, in which attention was directed at individual licensed premises which appeared to be associated with high numbers of violent incidents, but as time went on the project manager increasingly sought ways also to influence the wider social and commercial agenda.

---

1   Street robbery has recently received considerable attention elsewhere, particularly under the auspices of the Home Office Street Crime Initiative. It is worth noting that street robbery is relatively infrequent in central Cardiff, and that only a handful of robberies were identified in which there was any evidence of alcohol consumption by the offender.

Aims and approach of the TASC project

The initial project bid submitted to the Home Office outlined the following objectives:

- to enhance police intelligence by gathering data from a variety of sources, including Accident and Emergency records, in order to identify 'hot spots' for alcohol-related violence and disorder in Cardiff;
- to analyse these data to develop effective, innovative and creative solutions to the problems identified;
- to establish an effective multi-agency project;
- to establish a 'Licensees Forum', and strong and effective working relations with the licensees of all licensed premises in the City Centre;
- to provide a responsive and effective training programme for all who work in licensed premises in Cardiff, appropriate to their needs;
- to establish an awareness campaign to maximise the overall effect of the initiative;
- to encourage increased reporting of alcohol-related offences to the police; and
- to develop appropriate counselling services to challenge offending behaviour and prevent repeat offending.

As noted above, the initial focus of the project – and one which, despite increasing involvement in wider policy issues, remained strong throughout – was upon 'hot spots' of alcohol-related violence and disorder: in other words, upon small areas, streets or individual pubs or clubs which become the site of unusually high numbers of violent or disorderly incidents, especially late at night. In adopting this focus, the project was guided partly by previous research suggesting that such clusters are created by a variety of highly localised factors such as poor management or physical design of licensed premises (Graham and Homel, 1997), inadequate selection, registration and training of door staff (Deehan, 1999; Hobbs et al., 2000, 2002) and sudden gatherings of crowds at locations such as taxi ranks and fast food outlets when several pubs or clubs close at the same time (eg Purser, 1997).

It was decided at the time of the bid to focus exclusively on police sectors 29 and 30 (Cardiff City and Cardiff Bay area) where the majority of licensed premises are situated. The TASC team set out, first of all, to identify 'hot spots' within these areas. To assist in this process, it created a comprehensive database of all known incidents of 'alcohol-related crime and disorder' in the two sectors. This was continually updated and used throughout the life of the project to target police interventions and to persuade managers in premises with high rates of violence or disorder to co-operate in remedial plans (such as improvements in staffing, security or design). Of course, 'alcohol-related' and 'disorder' (and to a lesser extent, 'violence') are rather vague terms, and some arbitrary decisions had to be made about how they were to be defined and used in practice. This issue will be discussed later in this chapter.

The project team also adopted a variety of other strategies to meet its broader objectives, including sponsoring a new cognitive-behavioural programme for violent offenders with alcohol problems ('COV-AID') and launching a number of advertising and educational initiatives aimed at both drinkers and potential drinkers (especially young people). Perhaps most importantly for the long term, it attempted to raise awareness of alcohol related violence and disorder among those responsible for planning and licensing strategies in the city, and among senior managers in major leisure 'chains' and breweries.

Organisation, staffing and roles

The emergence of the TASC project owed a great deal to the prior work of the Cardiff Violence Prevention Group (CVPG). Established in 1997, and led since its inception by a prominent Cardiff surgeon, this was an inter-agency group set up to examine and devise preventive solutions to violence across Cardiff, mainly from a 'public health' perspective. The CVPG continued to work in this and other areas of violence, but on achieving Home Office funding the TASC project was set up as an independent multi-agency partnership. The partners were South Wales Police (lead agency), Cardiff County Council, Safer Cardiff, the Accident and Emergency Unit of the University Hospital of Wales, and the Cardiff Licensees Forum. Representatives of these agencies sat on a steering committee responsible for direction and oversight of the project. The Council was represented by the City Centre Operations Manager and the Operations Manager from Environmental and Public Protection. The Deputy Chair of the Licensing Magistrates was also a member.

The TASC offices were located in Cardiff Central police station, a situation which undoubtedly benefited the project by giving its staff direct access to key information sources, as well as to operational commanders responsible for decisions about the use of city centre policing resources. This contact was especially important in April 2000, when the administrative structure of South Wales Police underwent a major re-organisation and Cardiff became one division instead of three. The project team was also reassured on site that no problems would be encountered in collecting all relevant police data on the target sectors, both retrospectively and prospectively.

The TASC staff comprised a project manager (a police inspector), training sergeant, data analyst, administrator and project nurse (based in the A & E Unit). It was always the intention that the project manager appointed to TASC would be a uniformed officer of at least Inspector rank. This was because the overall objective of TASC was undoubtedly high profile and required the input of a senior officer experienced in dealing with the media and with city centre operational policing issues. The project manager was responsible for co-ordinating and managing the project and the team on a day-to-day basis, as well as for most of the liaison with operational police managers, senior managers of other organisations and the media.

The bulk of the contact 'on the ground' with pub and club managers was undertaken by the training sergeant, who visited them on a regular basis and encouraged those with high or rising violence rates, or whose door or security staff had a poor reputation, to initiate improvements. The sergeant maintained close links – and often undertook joint visits – with a team of four licensing officers who were based in the same building, and whose work was also regularly informed by the TASC database.

The data analyst's key role was to maintain and analyse a comprehensive database of information from a variety of police and hospital sources. The ongoing analysis of these data both informed decisions on which premises to target for interventions (including some sizeable policing operations) and provided a continuous monitoring process for the TASC project as a whole, allowing any new trends or emerging issues to be picked up at an early stage. While data collection exercises are not always seen as useful by operational staff, it will be shown later that in this case the database proved to be of central value to the work of the project, and was used for practical purposes on a frequent basis. It was also of major assistance to the evaluators, who were closely involved in its design from the beginning.

The nurse based in A & E performed two principal roles: first, to provide advice and support to victims of violence, where appropriate trying to persuade them to report assaults to the police; and second, to supplement the information in the TASC database with more details of the circumstances and locations of violent incidents (including assaults not recorded by the police). The latter role was performed on an anonymous basis unless the patient agreed to having their name or other details forwarded to the project.

Evaluation approach and methodology

The central purpose of the evaluation was to assess the impact of the TASC project in reducing alcohol-related violence and disorder in a small geographical area over the short term (i.e. during its lifetime as a TPI project). This meant that most of the systematic data collection and analysis undertaken was aimed at identifying any changes in the levels and patterns of relevant incidents in the targeted police sectors, looking both at the sectors as a whole and at individual 'hot spots' within them. Although this aspect of the study inevitably dominates the report, it should not be forgotten that other more general and less localised strategies were pursued by TASC to improve knowledge about alcohol problems and influence cultural attitudes over the longer term: for example, advertising campaigns, visits to schools and an offender programme. It is impossible to assess the crime reduction impact of these strategies at this stage, and they can be evaluated only in terms of the views and experiences of participants. The fact that their outcomes are less immediately apparent and less measurable in statistical terms does not, of course, mean that they are less effective or less important than the geographically targeted 'policing' interventions.

In addition to the abovementioned outcome evaluation, the research team set out to produce a 'process' evaluation of the project, addressing questions about the implementation of its various elements, about the development of partnership working (especially work with the private sector) and about the identification of 'good practice'. Finally, a systematic assessment was undertaken of the cost-effectiveness of the project.

The outcome evaluation and the TASC database

Where measurement of crime reduction outcomes is concerned, the basic approach adopted was to undertake comparisons of levels of 'alcohol-related violence and disorder' in police sectors 29 and 30 (Cardiff City and the Bay area, respectively), or in particular streets or licensed premises within these sectors, both before and after the commencement of the TASC project, and before and after specific interventions. The main instrument for these purposes was the TASC database which, as noted above, was designed to a large extent by the evaluators and maintained throughout the life of the project by the data analyst. This held detailed information about the time and location of relevant incidents, the apparent reasons behind them, any weapons used or injuries sustained, and the characteristics of victims and alleged offenders. Two key issues in designing this database, of course, were what sources of information should be used to compile it, and what exactly should be counted as 'alcohol-related violence and disorder'.

Data sources

In constructing the TASC database, the aim was to identify as many relevant incidents as possible, using a variety of sets of systematically collected information. The database was unusual in that it combined into one SPSS file data from several police sources and an outside source. The police sources were incident records, custody handling records, crime records, CCTV logs, and extra information obtained by the analyst directly from officers. These were supplemented by information from the hospital Accident and Emergency unit, where patients who said that they had been assaulted were asked by reception staff to give brief details on where and when the assault took place. Further detail was added by the project nurse, who systematically telephoned such patients to offer support or advice and at the same time gleaned extra information about the incident. The resulting information was passed to the analyst (in open or anonymous form depending upon victims' permission) and added to the database, where it was used to create a new incident record or to enhance existing records. In compiling the database, the analyst checked each record individually to ensure that cases from the different sources were not 'double counted'. She received sufficient information in the vast majority of cases to be confident that this had not occurred. In the few cases where she could not be sure, she did not create a new record.

In order to allow 'before and after' comparisons of patterns of crimes and incidents, the analyst entered equivalent data going back to 1 July 1999, thus providing comparable data for a 12-month period prior to any TASC-initiated interventions. As far as possible, this retrospective data collection was carried out in the same way as the prospective data collection (see below).

Definitional issues

Incidents qualified for inclusion in the database only if they fell within the definitions of 'alcohol-related violence' or 'alcohol-related disorder' adopted by the project. First of all, in keeping with the aims of the TASC project, information was collected only on incidents which occurred on the streets or inside licensed premises or fast-food outlets: 'domestic' violence occurring within private homes was excluded. 'Violence' was deemed to include any kind of physical assault (including robbery, but not 'snatch' theft or 'theft from the person'). 'Disorder' was defined as any event classified in police crime or incident records as involving a breach of the peace, 'disturbance', 'drunk and disorder', or actions falling under s4 or s5 of the Public Order Act 1986.

The trickiest definitional issue was to decide what should be counted as an 'alcohol-related' incident. It should immediately be made clear that no claim was or is made that the incidents included in the database were directly *caused* by alcohol. This is a complex issue, and some researchers have argued that many assaults by people who have been drinking are the result of factors other than the consumption of alcohol *per se* (see, for example, SIRC, 2002). Equally, no attempt was made to establish how much people had been drinking, or whether they could be described as 'intoxicated'. Rather, the focus of the project – and of the evaluation – was upon the reduction of violent and disorderly incidents which could be deemed 'alcohol-related' in a much wider sense, in that they not only involved people who had recently been drinking, but that they also occurred within an area of town – or inside premises – in which the consumption of alcohol was a prominent feature of the cultural environment.

This perception of the targeted 'problem' was translated into systematic recording practice by developing a few simple rules. First, cases were included if they had already been flagged in the police recording system as 'U16' (alcohol-related): however, officers were not always diligent in attaching this flag and there was clearly a degree of under-recording. Secondly, reports of assaults or disorder taking place inside or just outside named pubs or licensed clubs were assumed automatically to be alcohol-related. Of course, there will be a few cases in which none of the participants had actually consumed alcohol and a few in which the named premises had nothing at all to do with the incident. However, detailed examination of samples of cases included on the above criteria revealed that such exceptions were rare (most offenders had clearly been drinking, and particular premises tended to be named in police reports only when the person concerned had been inside them or had got into an altercation with their door staff). Thirdly, incidents occurring elsewhere were included if there was some *prima facie* evidence in the reports of the consumption of alcohol by offender, victim or both. And finally, in any case in which it appeared likely that alcohol had been involved (eg street assaults occurring in the late evening) but this was not certain from the available information, the analyst made persistent efforts to discover whether one or more of the participants had recently been drinking: most commonly, she sent a memo to the officer in the case asking for further details. Similarly, the project nurse chased up unclear cases via A & E records or through telephone calls or short postal questionnaires to victims. Both the analyst and (to a lesser extent) the project nurse carried out these inquiries retrospectively as well as prospectively, so that the figures for the pre-TASC period were based as far as possible on the same procedures as those for the period the project was in operation.

Of course, the above methods did not produce a 'fully accurate' record of 'alcohol-related' incidents of 'violence and disorder' in the targeted area. Not only were details of some cases never found despite the efforts of the analyst or nurse, and some cases missed entirely through inconsistent recording procedures (especially in the case of A & E data), but concepts such as 'alcohol-related' and 'disorder' are in themselves somewhat vague and subjective. Nevertheless, the method chosen was applied consistently, and the evaluators regard the resulting database as sufficiently robust for present purposes.

Data on interventions and environmental changes

The TASC database allowed detailed analysis of patterns of violence and disorder on a weekly basis, including examination of incidents in or outside particular venues. It could also be seen whether any apparent trends were echoed in data from *all* of the different sources or just in some. However, in order to see if such changes could be directly linked to the activities of the TASC project, or might have been influenced by other factors, it was necessary to collect systematic information about (a) interventions or operations undertaken by the TASC team and/or by other police officers; (b) changes in the environment (eg the opening of new licensed premises, or the hosting of major sporting events) which might affect the numbers or habits of people drinking in the city centre; and (c) general trends in violence and disorder in neighbouring or similar areas.

As will be discussed later, there was during the lifetime of the project a significant increase in the total customer capacity of pubs and clubs in the city centre, and in the numbers of people drinking there late at night. There were also several major new sporting and cultural events. These developments clearly increased the numbers of potential offenders and victims affected by alcohol (thus setting the TASC project the extra challenge of not simply *reducing* violence and disorder, but *stopping it rising*), but it is very difficult to estimate to what extent – had there been no TASC project and had all other factors remained unchanged – this potential would have been translated into reality.

Monthly statistics on violent incidents were obtained for the rest of Cardiff and for the South Wales area as a whole, in order to compare trends in the targeted area against those in surrounding areas (as well as to address the possibility of 'displacement': however, while displacement of violent behaviour from well regulated to less well regulated premises within the city centre is a clear possibility, displacement to other areas of the city – where there is no comparable 'entertainment area' – is considered unlikely).

Process and cost-effectiveness evaluations

The evaluators employed a variety of other research methods, mainly of a qualitative nature, to understand and evaluate process issues in the implementation of the project. These included frequent observation of the work of the project team (eg spending time in the office and accompanying the training officer on visits) and both formal and informal interviews with interested parties (eg managers of licensed premises, door staff, police officers). The main fieldworker spent a significant amount of time in the project office – often two or three days a week. This allowed a relationship of trust to develop whereby project staff could speak openly about any issues of concern. Project staff were regularly questioned about the development of the project and the rationale behind particular decisions and actions. All documentation was made available to the evaluators and copies were regularly prepared for them prior to their arrival in the police station. They were usually told in advance of important meetings and events, and accompanied project staff to many of these (eg visits to licensed premises, the hospital, door staff training events, Steering Group meetings).

Finally, the researchers from CRG collected and analysed data relevant to the determination of cost-effectiveness.[2] This involved:

- understanding the planned use of input resources and assigning measurable units of output (product) for each intervention[3];
- estimating the cost (on a quarterly basis) for all resources consumed in the project paying particular attention to variance from planned expenditure;
- comparing costs with impacts on alcohol-related violence and disorder; and
- comparing the result with the cost of the alternative under various assumptions.

---

2 Defined as the comparison of 'alternative cost streams to produce broadly similar outputs or outcomes' (Dhiri and Brand, 1999).

3 Here the term 'intervention' refers to the broad activities (described in more detail in Chapter 3) that form the TASC project.

2.   Implementation of the TASC project

The TASC interventions can be divided into eight main categories, most of which were planned from the beginning, but one or two of which evolved in the light of experience and through contacts with people with cognate interests elsewhere in the UK. They will be discussed in turn under the following headings:

- focused dialogue between the police and members of the licensed trade;
- measures aimed at improving the quality and behaviour of door staff;
- attempts to influence licensing policy and practice;
- measures aimed at publicising the problem of alcohol-related violent crime;
- targeted policing operations directed at crime and disorder 'hot spots';
- a cognitive behavioural programme for repeat offenders ('COV-AID');
- a training programme for bar staff ('Servewise');
- a programme of education about alcohol for school-age children; and
- support for victims of alcohol-related assaults attending hospital.

Focused dialogue between the police and members of the licensed trade

The Licensees Forum
Undoubtedly the most significant development in the TASC project at the start of 2000 – and arguably throughout the project – was the creation of a Licensees Forum in Cardiff. The TASC team was central to both setting up the Forum and ensuring its continuation beyond the planned end of the Home Office project in March 2002 (extra Home Office funding has allowed the initiative to continue to March 2003).

Plans for the creation of a Licensees Forum were first mooted in a meeting with a few interested licensees in October 1999. A month later, the TASC project manager sent letters to all licensees in Cardiff City and the Bay area inviting membership of the Forum. Although the initial response rate from licensees was poor (with only four replies from a total of 60 letters sent out), as time went on more saw the benefits of such a Forum and declared their interest in joining. The TASC project agreed to carry out all of the administrative support for the Forum (and did so throughout the life of the project) but always stressed to licensees that the Forum should be sustained after TASC had finished and that the group was effectively 'theirs'.

The Forum, the first meeting of which took place on 10 January 2000, had as its main aims the fostering of strong and effective relations between the managers of all licensed premises in the city centre, and the establishment of effective dialogue with the police, magistrates and council officials. Prior to its creation, most licensees in Cardiff had some contact with one another, but tended not to speak with 'one voice'.

Early dialogue was overshadowed by the controversial issue of 'naming and shaming', which caused a considerable degree of friction. This arose from a policy which had been adopted by the Cardiff Violence Prevention Group (CVPG) from October 1998, whereby it released to the local press 'league tables' of recent assaults in or outside individual named licensed premises, based on questionnaires completed in the A & E Unit of the hospital. Many managers were upset by the campaign, arguing that the monthly figures for any one establishment were too small to draw conclusions from, that the league tables were of dubious validity (for example, very large clubs were compared directly with small pubs), and that some of the incidents were not directly linked with the premises named. Although the naming and shaming practice was strongly opposed by the TASC project board – which sought a co-operative rather than a confrontational approach – when it was formed a year later, licensees did not always distinguish clearly between TASC and the CVPG, and initially many regarded TASC as an opponent rather than an ally.

The issue was resolved within a few months when the CVPG stopped supplying data to the press, a move which met with general approval. However, although the media campaign raised the hackles of most licensees and was seen by the TASC team as counter-productive, some beneficial results were apparent. It appeared to have a galvanising effect on pub managers and – however unfair it may have been – had it not taken place, there may have been less interest in joining the Forum and co-operating with TASC. This view was supported by one of the managers interviewed, who saw the value of a 'short, sharp' negative campaign to 'concentrate minds', followed by a more co-operative and partnership based approach.

Participation in the Forum has remained strong. Over 100 managers have become members, representing virtually all licensed premises in Central Cardiff, and meetings have taken place at regular intervals. Between January 2000 and December 2001, 15 formal meetings of the Forum took place, with attendance averaging around 20. Its success over this period was due in large part to the chairmanship of a very active bar manager (who also sat as a member of the TASC Steering Group). He played a major role in 'selling' the benefits of participation to others in the area, as well as to regional managers in some of the large 'chains' which own pubs and clubs in the city. In doing so, he stressed the commercial value to all traders of maintaining the reputation of Cardiff as a 'safe' city for an evening out. The chairman also maintained full and active links with South Wales Police and there is no doubt that this had a significant effect in improving relations and co-operation between the police and licensing community generally in Cardiff.

The Forum meetings developed in a way that permitted constructive dialogue between all licensees on issues that concerned them. In the early months, a variety of issues were discussed, including trouble associated with fast food outlets, the location of taxi ranks, the deployment of police during large sporting events, and the use of CCTV in licensed premises. Relations later developed to the extent that the Forum was routinely briefed by the police prior to major sporting events. On 8 August 2001, for example, a meeting took place between senior police officers and members of the Licensees Forum regarding the FA Charity Shield game between Manchester United and Liverpool. The meeting agreed ways in which the police and licensed premises managers could co-operate during the match, especially in providing intelligence on known 'trouble-makers', making use of the radio-net system to contact Cardiff Central police station in the event of trouble and using specific licensees as contact points when serious disorder occurred. Attendance at such meetings has been as large as 60 managers. The police and the Forum also reached an agreement that during major rugby matches, when substantial numbers of people drink outside pubs, all City centre premises would use unbreakable (Government stamed) glasses and would not sell beer in bottles. Bulk purchase of such glasses was arranged through the Forum.

Finally, in addition to its administrative support, the TASC project played an important part in maintaining police links with the Forum. The project manager and data analyst made frequent presentations to the Forum and attempts were always made to keep its members up to date with TASC project statistics and initiatives.

Visits by the TASC sergeant

A further important channel of communication between the TASC project and licensees was through the training sergeant, who made frequent visits to pubs and clubs to carry out informal inspections and to make recommendations about security. At first, these visits were on a fairly random basis. However, as the project progressed, they were closely targeted, using the TASC database to identify premises which had recently experienced significant violent incidents, or which had a higher than average violence rate over time. Also targeted were premises where concerns had come to light about the behaviour of door staff. The police licensing officers were kept informed of the visits to avoid duplication or mixed messages, and in some cases joint visits were made. Two examples of these interventions are given below, the first being essentially a 'routine' visit to a club which had experienced recent assaults, the second a series of visits to a club about which there were more concerns.

Example 1

In November 2001, a member of the evaluation team accompanied the TASC training sergeant on a visit to a club which had recently experienced a slight increase in its normally low assault figures (as shown in data provided by the TASC data analyst). On this visit, the sergeant advised on the advantages of using CCTV in the particular venue and having bar staff with adequate professional training. The visit was carried out in a friendly spirit and it was clear that relations between the police and the licensee were positive. The licensee commented on the benefits of having an identifiable individual within the police whom they could contact when needed.

Example 2

In November 2001, the sergeant carried out a number of visits to a night-club, accompanied on some by police licensing officers. The club in question had seen a sustained rise in violent incidents taking place both inside the club and outside in the street. Of particular concern to the police was a high number of violent incidents involving door staff employed at the club and the fact that in-house CCTV cameras were often not recording when such incidents occurred. An alleged assault by door staff (recorded on police CCTV in September) was, at the time, a matter for investigation by the police. The general manager of the club was informed that inoperation of his CCTV cameras was a breach of the entertainment licence. The general manager was asked to ensure that:

- in future, CCTV cameras in the premise be recording at all times;
- persons who are drunk are not admitted to the premise;
- members of his staff challenge under-age drinkers; and
- all door staff are trained and registered under the Cardiff Licensed Premises Supervisors scheme.

The meeting turned out to be essentially positive. The manager agreed to work with the police in reducing the numbers of assaults taking place in/near his club. The security company providing door staff also agreed to ensure that all staff provided would be trained under the Cardiff scheme.

Dialogue with senior management

In addition to meetings with individual pub and club managers, the TASC team made efforts to influence senior managers of major leisure companies and breweries. Perhaps the most successful of these concerned a particular club in which analysis of patterns of assaults suggested that its high rate of violence was partly caused by very cheap drinks promotions in 'happy hours': these were attracting large numbers of young people, many of whom were getting drunk in a short space of time. Having been told by the local manager that such promotions were 'company policy', the TASC manager contacted senior executives from the chain which owned the club and a series of high level meetings took place, involving also the Chief Superintendent from the Cardiff police division and licensing officers. Despite initial resistance, the company agreed under some pressure to stop the promotion.

A more ambitious initiative, to engage major companies in a broader and ongoing dialogue about strategies to reduce alcohol-related violence and disorder, had less tangible results. With the help of the Licensees Forum, a meeting was held in 2001 with 14 area managers from breweries and leisure companies. However, while they agreed to make individual efforts to improve security and staff training, the managers generally resisted more radical suggestions (such as co-ordinated reductions in drinks promotions) which might significantly affect profits. There was also little enthusiasm for setting up regular group meetings among what was essentially a group of competitors. The main positive result of the meeting was the opening of channels of communication between TASC and senior managers from individual companies, which proved useful on later occasions when the project identified rises in assaults or other problems in particular pubs or clubs: as well as discussing problems with the local manager, the TASC team was able to put its points at a higher level in the company. Overall, the TASC manager concluded that the commercial imperatives – strong competition for custom in a crowded market, and the need to maintain sales of alcohol at 'quiet' times as well as at weekends and during major events – were too strong to allow him more than a marginal influence on company policies.

Measures aimed at improving the quality and behaviour of door staff

In line with a number of other major cities with a large number of pubs and clubs, Cardiff has a similarly large population of 'licensed premises supervisors' – more commonly known as 'door staff' or 'bouncers' – employed to 'work the doors' of pubs and clubs: for example, around 700 were employed in April 2001. As in other cities (see, for example, Lister et al., 2001), the roles and behaviour of door staff have never been far from controversy. Quite high numbers have been arrested for assaults against members of the public or the police (see Chapter 3), and some have been suspected of drug dealing and other illegal activities. Before the creation of the TASC project, relationships between the police and the door staff 'community' were quite poor, the latter tending to resent 'interference' on what they regarded as 'their patch'. This 'them and us' situation had brewed in the background over several years with neither side having the resources (or the inclination) to fully confront some of the central issues. The TASC project was one of the first projects of its kind to identify these issues and systematically set about addressing them, principally through efforts to raise the standards of door staff and to give them a more 'professional' status.

Training and registration

The need to employ trained and registered door staff has for some years been formally required in central Cardiff under the conditions of licences for Public Entertainment for Music and Dancing ('PELs'), where it is stipulated that all security staff employed in relevant premises are trained and registered under the approved scheme. In reality however, there was little enforcement of this, and the training through which such licences were obtained took less than one day. One of the key planks of the strategy of TASC was the development of the Licensed Premises Supervisors Training Scheme, which delivered a new two-day training package to all door staff requesting a licence. The training incorporated an innovative conflict model and encouraged a sense of professionalism amongst door staff. The TASC project initiatives in this area also eliminated the situation whereby door staff could 'work the doors' whilst awaiting training. Temporary licences were abolished by the project, thus ensuring that door staff could only work if they were properly registered and trained.

Before the appearance of TASC, the training of door staff in Cardiff was largely the responsibility of the County Council, with minimal police involvement. In January 2000, the training sergeant on the TASC project conducted a substantial review of door staff schemes throughout South Wales and nationally. Police officers from Cardiff were invited to submit their own suggestions for the re-vamp of the Cardiff scheme. Recommendations were subsequently drawn up in a substantial document submitted by the project to the Head of Regulatory Services at Cardiff County Council. On the 16 February 2000, the project manager of TASC made a formal presentation to licensing magistrates and other representatives of the Licensing and Public Protection Committee. The recommendations proposed by TASC were far- reaching and can be summarised as follows:

- the implementation of measures designed to increase the administrative and operational efficiency of the scheme;
- abolition of the temporary registration scheme which permitted door staff to work whilst awaiting training;
- an increase in the length of the training from one day to two days, and placing it under police supervision;
- a new wider definition of a Licensed Premises Supervisor designed to bring greater numbers of 'fit and proper' individuals into the scheme;
- the introduction of a 'Code of Practice' for door staff to sign up to after training;.
- increase in registration fees from £25 to £100;
- immediate suspension of door staff in the event of obvious gross misconduct, especially offences involving violence or illegal substances (including steroids);
- police to investigate and deal with complaints about the conduct of door staff

- revisions to the penalty points system, especially an increase in the points given for offences of assault, police cautions for recordable offences, and for failure to attend court to give evidence in relation to incidents witnessed when on duty;
- a requirement for premises employing a registered LPS to display a notice to that effect;
- the introduction of random drugs testing for door staff; and
- the extension of the LPS scheme to *all* liquor licensed premises where door staff are employed – i.e. taking it beyond the scope of Public Entertainment Licences.

The County Council accepted the majority of the recommendations proposed by the TASC project. It did however reject the last two in the above list (on the use of random drugs testing and the extension of the scope of the schemes beyond PELs). The accepted revisions were eventually put in place in the autumn of 2000, at which time the Licensing Magistrate on the TASC Steering Group set up a meeting with some of the major door staff providers in Cardiff to inform them of the requirements of the LPS scheme in Cardiff and the need for co-operation with the police.[4] Between September 2000 and December 2001, 13 two-day training sessions took place, training an average of around 17 door staff each time.

Under TASC, the new training was backed up by closer police monitoring of instances where door staff infringed their membership of the LPSS (Licensed Premises Supervisors Scheme). The TASC project introduced a revised 'penalty' points system: an accumulation of 10 or more penalty points in any three-year period (when licences were renewed) would lead to an automatic revocation.

TASC also introduced a database of registered door staff. This includes photographs of door staff, a record of their penalty points and an up to date record of the pubs and clubs that they have worked at. Importantly, the TASC project office also became:

- the focus of several complaints against door staff by members of the public, which were dealt with promptly by the training sergeant;
- the main office where PNC checks were completed on potential applicants for criminal convictions; and
- a route for the referral to the Licensed Premises Supervisors Administration Committee (see below) of cases where door staff were involved in assaults or any other behaviour/s seen as contravening the LPS Code of Practice.

---

4   The Operations Manager from Environmental and Public Protection agreed that, in the event of problems with 'outside' security companies providing door staff to Cardiff premises, the Council would contact the security company and emphasise to them that all door staff employed in Cardiff had to be registered and trained under the terms of the new LPS scheme.

Implementation issues

Although the new scheme seemed quite strict 'on paper', in practice it was not always enforced with the speed, or to the degree, that the police, in particular, wished to see. This was apparent, above all, in the work of the Licensed Premises Supervisors Administration Committee, which took most of the key registration and disciplinary decisions. This Committee, which contained representatives from the main interested parties,[5] was responsible for considering applications from individuals who had convictions or cautions (and were thus prevented from automatically being accepted on to the registration and training scheme);[6] it also considered disciplinary matters that could lead to the revocation of a door supervisor's licence.

In 2001, 20 disciplinary cases were heard; six door staff licences were revoked; seven were refused; and 20 points for newly registered door staff were awarded. These figures were considered low by the TASC team, taking into account the numbers of door staff working in Cardiff (several hundred) and the numbers of complaints made about their behaviour. The team also pointed out that door staff frequently failed to attend the Committee hearings (when required to attend), in the knowledge that the proceedings would be adjourned in their absence. Given that the LPS Administration Committee only met once a month, cases often went unresolved for a considerable amount of time. Indeed, non-attendance was said by the team to be commonly used by door staff as a conscious delaying tactic, much to the frustration of the police.

This issue became a focus of friction between the police and the Council, and reflected some underlying differences of approach. Generally speaking, the police were keen to introduce and enforce strict measures that would ensure much tighter regulation of door staff than had previously been the case in Cardiff – including the permanent exclusion from local employment of door staff with histories of repeated violent conduct. The Council tended to take a more cautious line, and seemed on occasion slow to respond and opposed to strong action, even in cases where door staff had committed criminal offences. This caution was driven to a large extent by concerns about breaching human rights legislation and possible litigation.

The issue continued to raise its head throughout the whole of the evaluation period and beyond. For example, in the latter part of 2001, the Council advocated through their

---

5   The Committee comprised a Licensing Officer from the Council, a Licensing Committee member, a Police Officer, and representatives from the Licensing Magistrates, a licensed premise, a night-club, and the registered licensed premise supervisors. During the period of the TASC project, the training sergeant from TASC sat as the police representative on the Committee. In this way, police objections to the actions of particular door staff could be closely monitored and voiced at an early stage.

6   A rough points system, based on the frequency and severity of previous convictions, was devised to guide decisions on whether to accept applicants ('spent' convictions were not counted). Anyone rejected could re-apply at any time.

representative that a door supervisor who had committed a serious assault on a member of the public (captured on CCTV), be allowed to keep his registration badge pending a disciplinary appeal, and thus to keep working. The man repeatedly failed to attend any hearings and action on the matter was continually deferred by the Council's licensing representative. The police (and the chairman of the Licensees Forum) strongly objected to the Council's course of action and, in a letter, questioned whether the spirit behind the changes initiated by TASC were being fully supported by the Licensing Department of the Council.

Door staff reactions

It is probably not surprising that the increased regulation of door staff initiated by the TASC project met with objections from door staff themselves. The training sergeant from the project visited licensed premises on a regular basis to ensure that all staff 'working the doors' were properly trained and registered under the Cardiff scheme – prior to TASC this had never been done on a systematic basis. Merely turning up at the training (previously one day, under TASC two days) was no longer a guarantee of registration. As mentioned previously, TASC was also known by door staff to have initiated a much more stringent system of regulation aimed at ensuring that violent behaviour on their part would no longer be tolerated.

Representatives of door staff raised legal objections to the increased regulation by the police on two main counts, arguing:

(1) that they were being 'victimised' through the use of CCTV footage against them in disciplinary cases; and

(2) that the revocation of licences violated their basic right to work.

Following a long period of consultation with police solicitors, broad agreement was reached that use by the police of CCTV evidence in disciplinary matters was lawful. Support for this was established through Section 17 of the Crime and Disorder Act (1998), which states that local authorities and the police have an obligation to co-operate in the development and implementation of strategies for tackling crime and disorder. On the issue of revocation of door staff licences (preventing door staff from working), the police and Council argued that the LPS scheme and procedures adhered to the European Convention on Human Rights (Article 8), and that protecting the rights of individuals to work was balanced by the need to protect public safety.

In late 2000 and early 2001, 12 door staff from five venues were interviewed by the evaluators to obtain their views on the training and their relations with the police. All the venues held public entertainment licences and special hours certificates. All of the staff (two of whom were women) had completed the new LPS training.

The sentiments expressed by several of those interviewed showed that the long-standing poor relationships in Cardiff between door staff and the police still persisted to some extent. Five of the 12 thought that many police officers had a 'bad attitude' towards door staff, and a majority considered that the police had a tendency to believe the customer's side of a story rather than theirs. Comments about the police included:

'Police tend to believe the public.'

'We get harassed for licences all of the time.'

'Police should appreciate the environment that door staff work in.'

'Sometimes police are a pain. Some don't like door staff and always have an attitude.'

'It would be nice if door staff got some recognition of the work they do.'

'You could get away with giving someone a slap before but wouldn't now.'

On the other hand, the training course was reasonably well received. The most useful parts of the course were identified as the drugs and the first aid training, and to a lesser extent the session on their rights and the law. The main criticism made was that the training was 'too basic' (4 respondents).

Attempts to influence licensing policy and practice

As time went on, the TASC team became increasingly convinced that it should proactively set out to influence licensing policy and practice in the city, through the Council and the Licensing Magistrates. The database played a part in this, both by drawing the team's attention to a rapid growth in disorder in particular parts of the city centre (where, it concluded, there were simply too many licensed premises in a small area); and by providing a source of evidence in discussions with the Council and in legal challenges to new licences.

The main focus of its attention was one specific street, St Mary's Street, which had the highest density of pubs and clubs in the city and was experiencing a rapid increase in incidents of violence and disorder (see Chapter 4). The TASC manager, supported by senior officers and some members of the Licensees Forum, took the decision to oppose the granting of any new alcohol licences in this area, arguing that the city centre could not sustain such a high number of premises in a limited space.

However, despite the high profile of TASC, and despite using information from the database to support their argument, the police were largely unsuccessful in convincing licensing magistrates that granting such licences increased the potential for serious disorder in this area. They were also unsuccessful in an appeal to the Crown Court against the granting of a licence to open a new club in the location. The judge decided that it was not a properly brought case and commented that the police should 'get on with the job' of policing the area. The TASC team concluded that one of the main problems was that their objections were coming too late in the licence application process, and consequently decided to intervene much earlier, at the planning stage.

To this end, towards the end of the evaluation period, the TASC project manager and data analyst began exploratory discussions with the Council Planning Department. Arguments were put in terms of the Council's responsibilities under s.17 of the Crime and Disorder Act 1998 (i.e. that each local authority must 'exercise its various functions with due regard to the need to do all that it reasonably can to prevent ... crime and disorder in its area'), as well as pointing out the disadvantages of creating an unattractive area in the city centre in which most premises were locked up during the daytime. They also made presentations about the distribution of violent and disorderly incidents, using information from the TASC database. This had some impact, in the form of successful objections to an application to convert a commercial property in the street into a new nightclub. However, objections to planning permission for two other conversions in the area failed.[7]

At a more general level, the Chief Superintendent – supported by presentations from the TASC team – began to engage in meetings with the Council at executive level, arguing that a more planned and less piecemeal, 'laissez-faire' approach should be adopted towards the growth of licensed premises. This should include consideration of wider issues such as the density of population created in particular streets at particular times, and the availability of late night transport.

On the latter point, discussions extended to bus companies and representatives of taxi firms. These were successful in persuading Cardiff Bus to provide some late night services, based on a

---

7 Moreover, the TASC manager predicted that the first application would be resubmitted as a conversion to a licensed restaurant – and would then receive planning permission.

'cashless' system (brokered by the Licensees Forum), whereby bus tokens are sold in licensed premises during the evening. The discussions have so far been less successful in relation to taxis, where the main representative organisation has no control over the working policies or schedules of individual firms. A shortage of late night taxis in the city remains a considerable problem from the point of view of easing the build up of people on the streets after pubs and clubs close.

High level discussions of these kinds are continuing in an attempt to move the agenda beyond concerns about individual premises, into a much broader debate about crime and disorder issues in relation to the long-term planning and policy-making processes which will shape the future character of the city centre. Although there are considerable differences of viewpoint among key players, and no clear conclusions have yet been reached, the TASC project has undoubtedly played an important role in 'kick-starting' such a debate.

Measures aimed at publicising the problem of alcohol-related violent crime

The TASC project launched a number of advertising initiatives during the period studied. All were designed both to advertise the project and to highlight the issue of alcohol-related violence.

The official launch of TASC in June 2000 led to a fair amount of positive media interest, and the team continued to seek local publicity for its work. In all its communications, a strong emphasis was put on the value of a partnership approach in the reduction of violence. The TASC project developed its own poster and ran a prominent campaign advertising the project and 'safe drinking' on the sides of buses, on local radio and in the local press. The project manager and the training sergeant also gave 11 local radio interviews between them. This campaign ran over three periods, each of six to eight weeks, over Christmas 2000, Summer 2001 and Christmas 2001. These were chosen as times where there was expected to be a particularly high risk of alcohol related violence (although, as will be seen later, the summer months generally turned out to have lower than average incident rates). In May 2000, too, the project initiated its own website. This contained information about the project and its multi-agency background, as well as a questionnaire and link through which anyone who had been assaulted could report the incident to the police – if preferred, anonymously.

In December 2001, a final radio advertising campaign took place. The campaign involved the transmission of five (30 seconds) commercials promoting the message of 'safe drinking' over the Christmas period. TASC's radio campaign was supported by the distribution, through the Licensees Forum, of beer mats, posters and stickers throughout all licensed premises in Cardiff.

Targeted policing operations directed at crime and disorder 'hot spots'

A central objective of TASC was to use its database to pinpoint specific trouble 'hot spots' and, where feasible, to persuade police managers to mount appropriate operations. The two main operations that resulted from the process were approved by the Tasking and Co-ordination Group at Cardiff Central police station and both lasted eight weeks. They took place in July to September 2000 and January to March 2001. The operations will be briefly described here, and their outcomes discussed in Chapter 4. In both cases, the precise names and locations have been disguised.

Operation Alpha

The first operation involved concentrating police resources in one of the (then) most prominent violence 'hot spots' in Cardiff, a large dance club which we shall call Alpha. As part of the same operation, some similar actions were taken in relation to another major club situated in the city centre, 'Beta', but not on such a large scale. The data analyst provided information about the times and days when most incidents were occurring. The operation, which lasted from 14 July to 8 September 2000, was multi-pronged and combined friendly co-operation with the management and a 'harder line' approach. Its main components were as shown in box 1.

Box 1   Operation Alpha

- *High profile policing*. Additional police officers (32 officers working five hours overtime each between the hours of 10pm and 3am) were deployed at selected street locations, especially in the vicinity of the hot spot premises.
- *Dialogue with managers*. A frequent dialogue was established with the club's staff and management, keeping them informed of developments in the operation.
- *Monitoring of premises*. Regular visits were made by the TASC sergeant and the community constable to inspect CCTV facilities, dance and bar areas.
- *A proactive CID operation*. An operation targeting drugs misuse was mounted for one night, resulting in 10 arrests.
- *Door staff*. A presentation was made to the club's door staff about the TASC project objectives, and a meeting was held with the security company responsible for providing door staff at the club.
- *Police monitoring of door staff licences*. The Licensed Premises Supervisors Register was examined to ensure that all door staff had been properly trained under the LPS scheme and to check for any serious previous convictions.

> • *Late night dispersal of customers*: Consideration was given to reorganising the road layout to ensure that people attending the club could be quickly moved away from the area when it closed. Discussions were held with the Chair of Cardiff Hackney Association to plan for the relocation of the taxi rank outside the club, so that taxis could enter and exit more easily, avoiding possible conflict between people waiting for taxis. The management was also encouraged to alter the closing time to 4am, thus avoiding a congregation of young people on the street at the time other clubs were shutting (commonly between 1.30am and 2am).

Operation Gamma

A second substantial targeted policing operation – labelled here 'Operation Gamma'– took place between 17 January and 14 March 2001. This was a high visibility operation focused on two separate streets where there were a number of pubs and nightclubs and where, again, the database indicated high levels of violence and disorder. While some of the nightclubs were visited and given advice in a similar manner to Operation Alpha, in this case the attention was as much upon incidents occurring in the two streets as upon the individual premises situated there. The main aims of this operation were:

- to provide a high profile presence at both locations;
- to deter potential offenders and to pursue any complaints, providing an early resolution of incidents; and
- To minimise disruption to the general public.

It was modelled to a large extent on the earlier operation and involved the same number of police officers over a similar period. The police operation was mainly carried out at the peak period for violence and disorder – 10pm to 3am on Saturday nights – but partly also on Wednesday evenings, as this was a 'student night' in one of the big clubs which attracted large numbers of young people and was identified by the TASC data analyst as another high risk period and location for violence and disorder.

A cognitive behavioural programme for repeat offenders ('COV-AID')

In its initial bid to the Home Office, challenging the attitudes of offenders known to become violent under the influence of alcohol was identified as a central objective of the TASC project. This was to be achieved in partnership with the Probation Service through a new 'counselling service', although the form that this would take was not explicitly defined. Due principally to major reorganisation in the Probation Service, little action was taken in this direction until, somewhat fortuitously, a well-known psychologist who had developed a programme of this kind, and who had recently joined Cardiff University, happened to see the TASC project logo on a Cardiff bus. She approached the manager and offered to pilot the programme, called COV-AID (Control of Violence in Angry Impulsive Drinkers) under the TASC auspices.

In February 2001, this was agreed formally by the TASC Steering Group and, following refinements and further preparations, it was put into operation in July 2001. A researcher was employed by Cardiff University to deliver the programme. Initial recruitment on to the programme was slow but later picked up when posters and leaflets advertising the scheme were distributed amongst probation offices, Cardiff Central police station and the Crown/Magistrates Courts. A presentation was given on COV-AID to around 30 magistrates. All participants in the COV-AID programme (14 at the time of writing) have been referred through the courts as part of a community rehabilitation order: failure to comply with the programme leads to an individual's return to court.

COV-AID is a 10-session structured individual cognitive behavioural programme for offenders who have become aggressive after drinking. In line with the 'What Works' principles approved by the Corrective Services Accreditation Panel (formerly the Prison-Probation Service Joint Accreditation Panel), the programme uses cognitive behavioural techniques to promote a 'personal scientist' approach, whereby participants are encouraged to develop their own skills for cutting down on their drinking and controlling aggression. COV-AID is targeted towards men and women who have committed three or more acts of alcohol-related aggression in the last two years and who are assessed at medium/high risk of reoffending.

Clearly, given the short timescale and low numbers, it is impossible to evaluate the success or otherwise of the scheme at this stage. However, some general comments may be made about practical issues in its implementation.

Data received from the COV-AID researcher show that between August 2001 and March 2002, a total of 14 offenders were referred to the programme. At the end of March, the status of these 14 cases was as follows:

- Completed COV-AID   3
- In progress   2
- Imprisoned   3
- Not accepted   1
- Failed to attend first session   2
- Dropped out of course   2
- Waiting to start course   1

Despite strong efforts to promote and advertise COV-AID in Cardiff, referral on to the programme was slow. One limiting factor was that entry was restricted to referrals from the Cardiff area, because of the specific geographical remit of the TASC project. Other reasons identified were that:

- many repeat offenders are sentenced to prison rather than a community rehabilitation order, particularly where their offence is serious;
- as yet, COV-AID is not an accredited programme;
- offenders displaying alcohol problems are commonly referred to the Community Alcohol Team; and
- most alcohol-related violent offenders are 'first timers', rather than repeat offenders. This made them un-eligible for participation on a programme like COV-AID, which is targeted at high-risk offenders with long histories of alcohol abuse.

Moreover, the majority of those referred either did not start the programme or dropped out, for a variety of reasons including lack of basic literacy comprehension, re-arrest, admission to a psychiatric hospital and imprisonment. Of the three people who went through the whole programme, two took 3.5 months to complete the course and the third took approximately six months. Nevertheless, the two probation officers who were interviewed about it commented favourably upon the rehabilitative potential of the programme.

A training programme for bar staff ('Servewise')

In October 2001 – again, close to the end of the evaluation period – the TASC project launched 'Servewise', a training package for bar and hospitality staff purchased from the Scottish Council on Alcohol. The aim of the course is to set professional, responsible standards for anybody involved in the sale of alcohol. In Scotland, there is anecdotal evidence that it has been beneficial in increasing staff retention and decreasing incidents of violence and public order. Through the auspices of the TASC project, South Wales Police was the first police force outside Scotland to implement the programme (albeit tailored to suit the situation in Wales).

Although TASC purchased the permission to use Servewise, the programme was (and continues to be) delivered in Cardiff by the University of Wales Institute (UWIC) through its School of Hospitality, Tourism and Leisure Management. The course (costing £45) offers a comprehensive training programme to individuals who work in the hospitality industry. A maximum of 15 delegates can participate at any one time. Most pay the course fee themselves, although some are paid for by their employers. The course consists of two 3-hour units and covers topics such as licensing law, the physiological and psychological effects of alcohol, problem prevention, understanding aggression and strategies for the safe departure of customers from premises. The TASC project provided administrative support for the scheme through use of its administrative assistant, who sent out information and application forms for the scheme to pubs and clubs in Cardiff. A leading solicitors firm in Cardiff sponsored the publication of a 'Servers' Handbook' and contributed towards the cost of other promotional materials.

The initial purchase of the 'Servewise' programme was straightforward. However, some problems emerged when the programme became more well known in Cardiff, at which point its originators in Scotland began to seek more control over 'Servewise'. In correspondence copied to the evaluation team, the Scottish Council on Alcohol specified that the training programme should end when the TASC project finished. At the time of writing, contractual issues are still being worked out by solicitors representing South Wales Police and Alcohol Focus Scotland.

Such contractual issues aside, initial indicators are that the 'Servewise' initiative in Cardiff has been welcomed by licensees and others as long overdue. The first 'Servewise' course took place in October 2001 and 12 staff from a range of licensed premises took part. A further two sessions took place in November 2001. Subsequently, one of the largest nightclubs in Cardiff had half of all of their bar staff trained under the scheme. The benefits to club/bar owners appear to be obvious – the course is aimed at providing them with confident, informed, professional staff who develop a sense of pride about the job that they do. Brief informal interviews with pub managers and with people who attended the course produced unanimously positive replies. However, as the scheme got underway so late in the evaluation period, it has not been possible to evaluate it in any systematic way. It is hoped that this may be undertaken by UWIC at a later stage.

A programme of education about alcohol for school-age children

The 'Drinkwise' education programme, a 90-minute presentation on 'safe drinking' and the physical and emotional consequences of excessive alcohol consumption, was delivered under the TASC auspices to secondary schools throughout the Cardiff area. It was devised on the premise that school-age children are likely to be the customers of bars/clubs in future years and as such, need to be made aware of the consequences of abusing alcohol. The need for such a campaign was further reinforced by an early analysis of the TASC database, which showed that over five per cent of offenders in alcohol-related incidents were aged 17 years or under.[8]

8   When records covering 30 months were entered, the database indicated that, in cases where their ages were known, six per cent of offenders, and five per cent of victims, were aged 17 or younger. About 80 per cent of incidents with young offenders occurred in the street, rather than in licensed premises, which supports the view of some interviewees that drink bought from off-licences plays a part in the problem.

The schools package was put together by two South Wales Police community education officers in collaboration with the TASC training sergeant. In November 2000, 17 children aged 14 to 16 from a local High School attended a pilot presentation at Cardiff Central Police Station. The presentation was divided into a number of 'role play' scenarios, medical footage of assault injuries, a video presentation, and a discussion of alcohol measures through the use of a mock bar. The presentation (attended by the evaluators) created considerable interest among the children, and several questions and comments followed at the end of the session.

The programme was then 'rolled out', 27 further sessions being delivered during the evaluation period to pupils from all secondary schools in the city. It received very positive feedback from teachers, and there are plans to continue the programme in schools beyond the official end of the TASC project.

Support for victims of alcohol-related assaults attending hospital

As noted earlier, the project appointed a nurse, based at the A & E Department of the local hospital, who telephoned and interviewed victims of assault after they had been treated. The main aims of these interviews were threefold: to offer support services, to persuade victims (where appropriate) to report assaults to the police, and to obtain additional information about the locations and circumstances of incidents in order to strengthen the TASC statistical database. The latter was passed on in anonymised form to the TASC data analyst.

The Assistant Manager of the A & E Unit provided the project nurse with a print out of all assault patients' names and telephone numbers. Patients were given written information at the time of their treatment that they might be contacted by her, and if they did not formally decline within 72 hours, she contacted them by telephone. If she failed to make contact in several calls, they were sent a questionnaire by post. The standard telephone call included the administration of a short questionnaire, aimed at improving the quality of the TASC database (for example, confirming the location and that the assault was alcohol-related); a short PTSD (post-traumatic stress disorder) questionnaire; and offers of referral to Victim Support and other service organisations. Respondents indicating 'high' on their PTSD scores were re-contacted at intervals of a couple of days, one month and then six months. After one month, appropriate patients were offered an appointment at the PTSD clinic (held each Friday and attended by the project nurse, two psychologists and two psychiatrists).

Between June 2000 and March 2002, the project nurse contacted 750 people. Around 275 of these were referred to various Victim Support branches in the South Wales area. In light of this significant addition to the workload of Victim Support, the TASC project paid about £1,000 towards the training of 20 new VS volunteers.

The evaluators interviewed the project nurse at several points in the project to establish how the work was progressing. She reported that there had been no strong objections to the process on confidentiality grounds, and that patients had been highly positive about the service. On the other hand, the numbers of people agreeing to report previously unreported assaults were very small: most wished not to involve the police (a dedicated telephone line to the police installed in the A & E department for use by victims likewise generated very few calls).

Finally, two important practical conclusions reached were that it was not necessary to employ such a senior grade of nurse to gain additional information for the TASC project, and that the position did not need to be a full-time one.

Summarising comments on implementation

The implementation of most elements of the TASC project was in line with its initial aims and plans. The operational 'targeted policing' elements were particularly impressive in scope (their impact is discussed in Chapter 4), mainly due to the close collaboration of the TASC manager and analyst with key members of the divisional Tasking and Co-ordinating Group, so that the divisional commander was persuaded to sanction major operations over substantial periods in relation to violence 'hot spots'.

The 'Servewise' training programme for bar staff, the 'Drinkwise' educational programme for schools, the general TASC advertising campaigns, and the services for victims provided by the project nurse, were also all implemented efficiently and were commented upon favourably by most of the interested parties interviewed by the researchers. The implementation of the COV-AID offender programme was less successful, due to practical problems of referral and attrition, but the programme itself received positive comments from probation officers.

The reforms aimed at improving the professionalism of door staff constituted perhaps the most complex elements of the project to set up and administer, and came up against some obstacles (see below). However, by the end of the project, the training and registration elements of the new system were operating effectively, and progress was being made with the disciplinary system.

Overall, it was concluded that the three most important factors driving the successful implementation of the project were:

- Appropriate staffing levels and skills: most importantly, the full-time employment of a project manager of appropriate rank and experience, an experienced training sergeant and a skilled data analyst, all of whom played key roles to a high standard.
- An excellent working relationship with the Licensees Forum, which provided an important channel of communication to local club and pub managers (and to some extent to regional and national managers of breweries and leisure companies).
- The construction of a comprehensive, detailed and carefully maintained database of all known incidents of alcohol-related violence and disorder in the targeted area.

Conversely, the two main obstacles which hampered or delayed the project's effective working were early confusions of roles and responsibilities and slow progress with more strategic, partnership-based approaches.

Early confusions of roles and responsibilities

Identification of the relevant points of contact within particular organisations was not always clear at the start of the project, causing delays in initiating activities. This applied to some extent to the Council, the Probation Service and the hospital. These points of contact could have been identified more clearly before the project began. In addition, confusion about the role of the Cardiff Violence Prevention Group, and poor communication between it and the TASC project, caused problems early on, especially in relation to the CVPG's 'naming and shaming' campaign.

Slow progress with more strategic, partnership-based approaches

While the project achieved many of its aims in relation to dialogue with and reform of individual licensed premises, it was less successful in developing more strategic 'solutions' to alcohol-related problems in the city centre. Most of the initiatives were essentially police led, and at times it could be said that some of the other partners did not show the desired speed or enthusiasm in assisting planned reforms. This was particularly true of the County Council in relation to disciplinary measures against unsatisfactory or violent door staff and, more broadly, in relation to attempts to develop more strategic approaches to the management of late night activities in the city centre. The dialogue with regional and national managers of large companies involved in the 'late night economy' was also less fruitful than initially hoped.

3. Patterns of violence and disorder in the city centre

This chapter provides a statistical overview of patterns of street violence and disorder in the city centre, including the main locations of incidents, the times at which they occurred, the characteristics of those involved, the kinds of injury suffered, and some of the apparent reasons behind them. It is based primarily on the TASC database, which, as outlined earlier, combines data from a variety of police sources and from the A & E unit at the hospital. The period covered is July 1999 to December 2001.

The picture from the combined TASC database

Locations and times of incidents

The locations of most incidents were recorded according to the name of the street or the premises in or outside which they occurred. This allowed fairly precise 'hot-spotting' of the incidents, including regular monitoring of violence and disorder rates for particular premises. Although not used routinely by the TASC team, some experimentation was carried out with visual representations of the geographical distribution of incidents by means of GIS mapping techniques. An example showing just one month's incidents is reproduced in Appendix A. As can be clearly seen, the most concentrated clustering of incidents was in St Mary's Street, especially at its southern end, where licensed premises are more densely grouped than in any other part of Cardiff.

As Table 3.1 shows, over half the incidents were associated with specific licensed premises, in that they occurred either inside (30%) or just outside (21%) a named pub or club (nearly all those recorded as outside such premises either involved door staff or were thought by the police to have started inside). Most of the rest took place elsewhere on the streets. However, as will be shown later, there was a significant difference in pattern between incidents of disorder and those involving assaults.

Table 3.1   Locations of alcohol related incidents

	N	%
Associated with named licensed premises:		
Inside	1,444	30
Outside	1,010	21
N/k in or out	262	5
Associated with non-licensed premises:		
Inside	238	5
Outside	100	2
N/k in or out	2	-
Elsewhere in street	1,624	34
Train/bus station	109	2
No location recorded	3	-
Total	4,792	100

Figure 3.1   Incidents of violence and disorder by day and time
By day

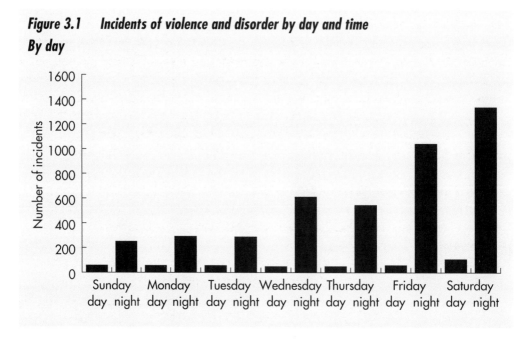

By time

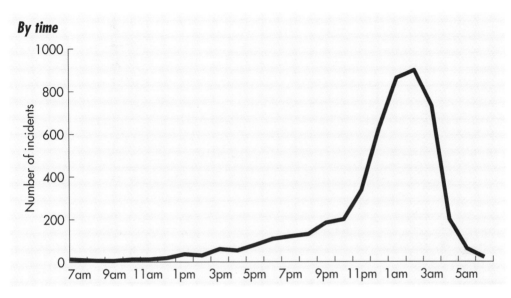

Offences were heavily concentrated not just in space, but also in time. Table 3.2 divides the week into 14 periods, showing the total number of incidents of violence and disorder recorded as having occurred in each period (the data cover the 30 months between July 1999 and December 2001). The table is also presented as a histogram in Figure 3.1. 'Daytime' is defined as 6am to before 6pm, and 'evening/night' as 6pm to before 6am. It can be seen that the great majority (91%) of incidents occurred during the evening or night and that, as one might expect, the highest concentrations of incidents of both crime and disorder occurred on Friday and Saturday nights, when the largest numbers of people congregated in clubs and pubs in the city centre (many of them not leaving until the early hours of the morning). Indeed, between them, *Friday and Saturday nights accounted for very nearly half of all known incidents.*

Table 3.2   Periods of week during which incidents occurred

	N		N
Sun daytime	57	Sun eve/night	250
Mon daytime	56	Mon eve/night	291
Tue daytime	56	Tue eve/night	287
Wed daytime	48	Wed eve/night	611
Thur daytime	49	Thur eve/night	545
Fri daytime	58	Fri eve/night	1,041
Sat daytime	107	Sat eve/night	1,336
Daytime total	431	*Eve/night total*	4,361

It can also be seen from the graph in Figure 3.1 that the city centre tends to be relatively 'safe' from early morning until well into the evening, and that the violence and disorder are squeezed mainly into quite a short period. As many as 65 per cent of all incidents took place in the four-hour period between 11pm and 3am. Moreover, it was this same short period on Friday and Saturday nights which saw by far the highest concentrations of incidents: the two four-hour periods of 11pm to 3am on Friday and Saturday nights, which between them make up under five per cent of the hours in a week, saw well over a third (36%) of all incidents. (Looked at another way, there were over 40 times more incidents during these hours on Saturday nights than on Wednesday afternoons).[9]

Characteristics of suspects and victims

As Table 3.3 shows, those arrested for alcohol-related violence or disorder were predominantly young white males (around half aged between 20 and 30), most of whom came from Cardiff or neighbouring Barry. The majority were first offenders, although one in five had at least four previous convictions. A substantial minority (15%), moreover, had been arrested for violent or public order offences four or more times in the past. A high proportion (54%) were unemployed or in unskilled manual jobs, but there were also significant numbers of students and people in clerical or professional jobs. In addition, 61 door staff were arrested over the 30-month period.

Assault victims whose details were recorded had fairly similar profiles to offenders in terms of age, sex and residence. Their occupations were generally not recorded, and it is not known how many had previous arrests or convictions. However, at least 110 of the 2,243 known victims of assault were door staff and 28 were police officers.

Data on the relationships between assailants and victims are missing in nearly two-thirds of cases, so not much reliance can be placed upon the findings in this area. For what it is worth, in cases where the relationship is known, about three-quarters of assaults involved strangers, rather than acquaintances, family or friends.

---

9   Over the 30-month period, there was a total of 934 incidents recorded for 11pm to 3am on Saturday nights. The total numbers of incidents on weekday afternoons (1pm to 5pm) ranged between 34 (Mondays) and 21 (Wednesdays).

Table 3.3   Characteristics of arrested persons and victims

	Arrested persons		Victims*	
	N	%	N	%
Male	2,445	88	1,863	83
Female	337	12	380	17
Under 20	639	23	518	23
20–29	1,371	49	1,174	52
30-39	520	19	413	16
40–49	155	6	100	4
50 or over	97	3	16	1
Not known	0	0	22	1
White	2,516	90	1,461	65
Afro-Caribbean	162	6	46	2
Asian	64	2	50	2
Other/NK	40	1	686	31
Resident in:				
Cardiff and Barry	1,869	67	1,160	52
Other SE Wales	482	17	230	10
Other Wales	74	3	30	1
England	48	2	68	3
NFA	46	2	0	0
Overseas	6	-	10	-
Other/not known	257	9	745	33
Unemployed	1,086	39		
Employed manual	724	26		
Employed clerical/professional	454	16		
Student/school	320	12		
Door staff	61	2		
Other/not known	137	5		
Previous convictions				
None	1,457	52		
1–3	760	27		
4–6	210	8		
7 or more	355	13		
Previous arrests for violence/PO				
None	1,614	58		
1–3	757	27		
4–6	188	7		
7 or more	223	8		
Totals	2,782	100	2,243	100

*Includes all victims on whom details were recorded, whether or not an offender was arrested.

Nature and circumstances of the incidents

It was often not possible to determine how or why incidents had arisen, but there is sufficient information to sketch a crude profile of some of the incidents and to throw a little more light on the overall picture of alcohol-related violence and disorder in Cardiff.

An important finding to note first is that the majority of incidents involved only one or two individuals; among the 3,166 cases where relevant information was recorded, only 770 (24%) involved three or more people and only 254 (8%) involved five or more. Equally, only 161 (7%) of the 2,286 cases in which arrests were made involved the arrest of more than two people, and relatively few incidents (4%) led to more than two criminal offences being recorded. This suggests that late night violence and disorder is mainly a problem of one-to-one confrontations or individual misbehaviour, rather than mass fighting or disorder.

To examine the incidents more closely, they were first divided broadly into cases of 'violence' and 'disorder'. This is a difficult distinction to make and some minor anomalies were apparent in the data (for example, some incidents were classified by the police as disorder, but resulted in arrests for assault). However, as a general rule, if there was any clear evidence of an assault having taken place – for example from hospital data or other police records – the incident is defined here as a violent one, even if the police recorded it as 'disorder'. Otherwise, the police classification has been retained. In addition, all incidents which were reported by A & E (and thus involved injury) but were *unknown* to the police, have been classified as 'violence'.

Based on the above method of classification, 61 per cent of all known incidents emerge as 'violent', and 39 per cent as simply 'disorder'.

Further analysis shows that there are some significant differences in the circumstances of the two types of incidents. First of all, the incidents of 'disorder' were less likely to involve groups of people. For example, only six per cent of all disorder incidents (80 cases) involved three or more people, compared with 37 per cent of all violent incidents (690 cases). This is of course a somewhat misleading finding, in that virtually all of the latter cases could be said to have involved disorder *as well as* violence. It may, however, suggest that melees in the street on a scale sufficient to attract police action are unlikely to pass off without some violence ensuing. Be that as it may, the most striking finding in this context is that over three-quarters of the incidents of 'disorder' involved only *one person*. The typical case appears to have been an individual who had drunk too much and become abusive or a nuisance.

Secondly, as Table 3.4 shows, violent incidents tended to be directly associated with particular clubs and pubs, while incidents of disorder more often took place on the streets. Indeed, 82 per cent of all incidents inside licensed premises involved assaults, compared with 57 per cent of those in the street outside particular licensed premises, and 47 per cent of those elsewhere in the streets. The proportionately low level of disorder 'inside' in comparison with 'outside' may again be partly the result of reporting and recording practices: it may be that the police are not usually called to incidents of disorder inside pubs and clubs unless they have led to assaults; or that, even if they are called, security staff have usually manoeuvred the 'troublemakers' outside by the time the police arrive (so that the incident is recorded as occurring outside, although it began inside). Even so, it is noteworthy that, among all alcohol-related incidents which resulted in somebody going to hospital, at least 40 per cent occurred inside licensed premises, and a further 20 per cent just outside them (see Table 3.5). In other words, it seems clear that the majority of the more serious violent incidents happened in and around particular pubs and clubs, rather than elsewhere on the streets.

Table 3.4   Types and sites of incidents

	Inside pubs or clubs	Outside pubs or clubs on streets	Elsewhere	Other/NK	Total
Incidents of disorder	303	432	908	216	1,859
Violent incidents	1,141	578	816	398	2,933
Total	1,444	1,010	1,724	614	4,792

Table 3.5   Locations of incidents leading to hospital visits

	N	%
Inside licensed premise	704	40
Outside licensed premise	343	20
Elsewhere in street	418	24
Other/Not known	287	16
Total	1,752	100

Another important finding is that security staff (or 'door staff') were involved in a substantial minority of incidents, especially *violent incidents inside licensed premises*. Thirty-four per cent (392) of the 1,141 violent incidents which took place inside licensed premises involved such staff. Most of these, moreover (at least 273 out of the 392), entailed allegations of assaults *by* door staff rather than *on* them. Door staff were additionally involved in 95 violent incidents in the street or elsewhere, mainly outside the premises where they worked (again more often as alleged assailants rather than as victims), and in 142 incidents of disorder (mainly 'altercations' over entry or ejection from premises). Overall, they were involved in at least 16 per cent of all known alcohol related violent incidents and eight per cent of all known alcohol-related incidents of disorder in the central Cardiff police sectors. To what extent such incidents were either avoidable or actually instigated by the door staff, of course, cannot be determined from the data. However, as noted earlier, 61 arrests of door staff were carried out over the 30 months, averaging out at two per month, or in one in ten of the incidents of violence or disorder in which door staff were recorded as having some involvement.

As Table 3.6 shows, there is no strong indication of the circumstances of most of the remaining incidents, although about a third of those involving assaults were described specifically as 'fights', suggesting that the 'victims' may not always be blameless. It is also worth briefly drawing attention to some of the smaller categories. So-called 'hate crime' appeared to be relatively unusual in this area of Cardiff, in that only 34 racial and 10 homophobic assaults or incidents were recorded. However, this is by no means a safe conclusion to draw, as previous research suggests that such incidents tend to be heavily under-recorded (see, for example, Phillips and Bowling, 2002). There were also 97 'domestic' assaults or incidents (i.e. those involving partners) in licensed premises or in the street, and 21 assaults on or altercations with, taxi drivers.

Table 3.6   Profile of types of incident

	N
Violent assault (unclassified)	1,744
'Fight'	839
Drunken disturbance/disorder	1,375
Alleged assault by door staff	332
Alleged assault on door staff	101
Other violence/fight involving door staff	54
Dispute/disorder involving door staff (eg customer refusal to leave)	142
Assault/fight/dispute with taxi driver	21
Domestic assault/fight/dispute	97
Racial incident/assault	34
Sexual incident/assault	43
Homophobic incident/assault	10
Total	4,792

Types of violence and injuries

Table 3.7 shows that by far the largest proportion of the incidents in which physical violence was used involved punches or kicks. The use of knives was relatively rare, but bottles or glasses figured in 10 per cent of attacks.

Table 3.7   Assaults: type of violence used

	N	%
Bodily force	363	12
Punch/kick	1,355	46
Bottle/glass	287	10
Knife	25	1
Other/not known	903	31
Total incidents with violence	2,933	100
(No physical violence)	(1,859)	

Among the 2,243 people who were known to have been assaulted (or who were injured during incidents of disorder), the most common injuries sustained were bruises and minor cuts. However, 15 per cent suffered broken bones and 12 per cent major cuts requiring stitches (see Table 3.8). Seventy-three per cent had facial, neck, head or teeth injuries – facial injuries being by far the most common. From reading accounts of the cases, the TASC analyst rated the injuries to two victims as life-threatening, and to 675 (30 % of all those assaulted) as 'severe'.

Finally, from what is known from police and A & E records, 65 per cent of all violent incidents (i.e. excluding those recorded as 'disorder') led to at least one person going to hospital. Altogether 1,973 people went to (or were taken to) hospital as a result of their injuries.

Table 3.8   Types and sites of injuries sustained

	N	%
Minor cuts/bruises/blows	1,215	54
Major cuts (stitches)	277	12
Broken bones	337	15
Bites	59	3
Severe blow	32	1
Knife wounds	8	-
Other/not visible/NK	315	14
Total	2,243	100
Face/neck/head/teeth	1,628	73
Arms/legs/hands	253	11
Trunk/abdomen	67	3
Whole body	35	2
Other/not known	260	2
Total	2,243	100

Alternative pictures: police and A & E data

The discussion in this chapter has so far been based upon the whole TASC database, which includes cases of both assaults and disorder, and combines a variety of sets of police data with information from the hospital's A & E Unit. The remainder of the Chapter will be devoted to an analysis of the various components of this database, in order to compare the pictures of alcohol-related crime and disorder painted by each. This is of topical importance, as considerable Home Office interest has been shown both in incident data (or 'calls for service') and in hospital data as alternative sources of information about trends in violent crime to the standard crime statistics (see, for example, Simmons, 2000).

Table 3.9 shows the numbers of incidents[10] identified from each of the four main data sources used: police *incident records* (i.e. mainly records of calls to the control centre), police *custody records* (i.e. records made when people are arrested and brought to the police station), police *crime records* (i.e. officially recorded offences) and statistics from the hospital *A & E Unit* (based on questionnaires to patients, supplemented by further

---

10 As explained earlier, the figures refer to 'incidents' or 'events', rather than 'crimes': a single incident can produce several offences. The incidents are subdivided into 'violence' and 'disorder' on the basis described earlier in this chapter.

information from the project nurse).[11] The table also shows how many of each set of incidents involved one or more offences that were 'crimed' – i.e. officially recorded as criminal offences of violence or against public order.

Table 3.9   Total numbers of alcohol-related incidents in central Cardiff, July 1999 to December 2001, according to four main data sources

| | Type of incident | | | | | |
| | Violence | | Disorder | | All incidents | |
Data source	N	Crimed	N	Crimed	N	Crimed
Incident records	2,163	1,030	1,268	522	3,431	1,552
Crime records	1,391	1,391	1,118	1,118	2,509	2,509
Custody records	1,006	894	1,158	1,045	2,164	1,939
A & E	1,689	758	9	1	1,698	759
Total incidents	2,933	1,323	1,859	972	4,792	2,295

N.B.   The totals are smaller than the sum of their columns, as many incidents were recorded in more than one data source (see next table).

Table 3.10   Overlaps between sources of data

Source of data	Number of incidents of crime or disorder	Number of violent incidents	Number of incidents with crimed assaults
Incident records	3,431	2,163	1,030
In custody/crime but not incident records	951	360	340
Total in police records	4,382	2,523	1,370
In hospital records but not police records	410	410	(potentially 410 extra crimes)
Totals of known incidents	4,792	2,933	1,370 (potentially 1,780)
% of incidents added by A & E data	9%	16%	30%

11 CCTV logs were used to supplement data from other sources, not as an independent source of new incidents.

It can be seen that the highest number of cases (3,431) appeared in the police incident records. Trawls of crime records and custody records threw up 2,509 and 2,164 incidents, respectively (if more than one person was arrested in relation to the same incident, only one incident was counted). Most of these were found in both sets of records, and many of them, too, had already been identified in the incident records. However, as Table 3.10 shows, the two new sources together produced a further 951 cases not identifiable in the incident records, bringing the total number of incidents identified from police sources to 4,382. Finally, the grand total was boosted to 4,792 by the inclusion of another 410 violent incidents identified from the hospital data but not identifiable in any of the police records.

At first glance, it does not appear that the hospital data add a great deal to what is already known from police records. Not only were 76 per cent of the 1,698 cases reported by the hospital already in police records, but the 410 'new' incidents increased the total of 'known' incidents by only 9 per cent (from 4,382 to 4,792). However, it has to be remembered, first of all, that the police figures include a large number of incidents of public disorder not resulting in injury, which one would not expect to result in visits to hospital. If we look only at incidents resulting in *assaults* (see column 2 of Table 3.10), the hospital data add *16 per cent* to the police-derived total. This figure rises to *30 per cent* if the comparison is made only with incidents involving at least one crimed offence of assault (column 3). In other words, *if every one of the 410 'new' incidents identified by the hospital were reported to and recorded by the police as an assault, the official crime figures for this type of offence would rise by around 30 per cent.*[12]

Summary

Alcohol-related incidents were very heavily concentrated in time and space. Friday and Saturday nights between them accounted for nearly half of all incidents. Indeed, the four-hour periods 11pm to 3pm on these nights together accounted for well over a third of the total.

Over 60 per cent of all known incidents involved physical violence, the remainder being incidents of 'disorder'. Most of the former involved only two people, and most of the latter involved single individuals who were 'drunk and disorderly': large scale 'mêlées' were unusual.

12 It has to be remembered that in the present study the comparison being made is with a very specific sub-group of violent incidents – namely, those involving alcohol-related assaults occurring on the street or in licensed premises in two Central Cardiff police sectors: it may well be that the 'dark figure' for other types of violence such as domestic assault is larger, and that hospital data would reveal a considerably greater proportion of hidden offences in these other areas. This would certainly be consistent with some older findings in Bristol by Shepherd, et al, (1989).

Well over half of all incidents were associated with individual licensed premises, occurring either inside them or in the street directly outside them. There was a considerable difference here between incidents involving assaults and those involving only disorder. While nearly 40 per cent of the former were recorded as taking place *inside* pubs or clubs, this was true of only 16 per cent of the latter. However, this may be an artefact of recording practice, as it is likely that, unless an assault has been committed, most inebriated people will be simply ejected on to the street by security staff, and the police will not be called to the pub or club.

Most of those involved as assailants or victims were young white males. The majority of those arrested had no previous convictions, but 42 per cent had been arrested previously for violent or public order offences.

'Door staff' were involved as victims or as alleged assailants in 16 per cent of all incidents involving violence, and in over a third of all such incidents taking place inside pubs or clubs. In a substantial majority of these cases they were the 'assailant' rather than the 'victim' (although of course this does not necessarily mean the assault was unprovoked or constituted a criminal offence). Altogether 61 door staff were arrested over the 30-month period examined.

The most common form of violence used was by punching or kicking; the use of knives was relatively rare, although at least ten per cent of assaults involved the use of bottles or glasses. Most injuries were fairly minor cuts and bruises to the face or head, but 15 per cent of victims of assault suffered broken bones and 12 per cent major cuts requiring stitches. Nearly two-thirds of violent incidents led to a hospital visit. Altogether, the TASC analyst categorised 30 per cent of assaults as 'serious'; two cases were classified as 'life threatening'.

Finally, it appeared that the majority of alcohol-related assaults identified through questionnaires at the hospital were already known to the police through one or other of their record systems (especially incident records). However, it was estimated that if all those not already reported to the police were now reported and recorded as offences, this would add about 30 per cent to recorded offences of this kind.

4.   Crime reduction outcomes

It is now time to move to the key question to be addressed in the evaluation: is there any evidence that the TASC project had an impact in terms of its core aim of reducing alcohol-related violence and disorder in its target area of central Cardiff?

This question will be addressed in two main ways. First, analysis will be conducted of trends in assaults and disorder (measured in a variety of ways) in the target sectors, both in the year before the TASC project was launched and during its implementation (especially during its first year, when direct 'before and after' comparisons can be made). It will be important also to compare these with trends elsewhere in South Wales, as well as to take into account the rapid growth of this part of Cardiff as a focal point for late night entertainment – a development which might in itself be expected to generate some increases in alcohol-related violent and disorderly behaviour. Second, a closer look will be taken at specific interventions in specific locations within the sectors, identifying any short or long term impacts that these may have had at a highly localised level.

Changes in violence and disorder in the target sectors

Figure 4.1 represents all known incidents involving violence and disorder (without physical violence)[13] between July 1999 and December 2001, measured at two-monthly intervals (Appendix Table B shows the same data in tabular form). It can be seen that there was a considerable difference in pattern between the two types of incident. The basic pattern for *disorder* was a substantial rise in the late summer and autumn of 2000 – i.e. shortly after the launch of the TASC project in July – and the maintenance of a fairly high level thereafter. Incidents involving *violence*, by contrast, showed a strongly seasonal pattern (with assaults rising towards the end of each calendar year and falling towards the early summer), but overall a slight fall during the first 12 months of the project. Specifically, the first 12 months after the launch of the project saw a *49 per cent increase in incidents of disorder* compared to the previous 12 months; *for violence, the equivalent figure was a fall of four per cent.*

The above difference in trends is confirmed by all the available police sources of information: for example, for incidents involving disorder only, the three main record sources – incident data, crime records and custody records – indicated rises varying

---

13 Definitions of 'violence' and 'disorder' have already been given in Chapter 1.

between 53 and 68 per cent, while for incidents involving assaults, they varied between a fall of 12 per cent and a tiny rise (see Table 4.1). Appendix Figures B.1 and B.2 also indicate that there was not a major change in police recording behaviour, at least in terms of the proportions of incidents that they 'crimed': for both violence and disorder, incidents involving recorded offences moved in a similar pattern to all known incidents.

The figures obtained from A & E, of course, refer only to incidents involving assaults. Overall, these paint a somewhat different picture of trends in violent incidents, indicating a 16 per cent *rise* between the pre-project year and the first year of the project, in contrast to a two per cent fall indicated by all police data combined.

However, it is quite likely that this rise is to a large extent artificial, brought about mainly by more efficient data collection in the hospital (including the activities of the project nurse). A related point of interest is that, if one looks only at A & E cases *not known to the police*, a fall of 16 per cent is indicated. This could reflect some success by the nurse and others in A & E in persuading patients to report assaults to the police – one of the objectives of that section of the project.

Figure 4.1 **Incidents of violence and disorder, central Cardiff, July 1999 to Dec 2001**
Incidents of violence

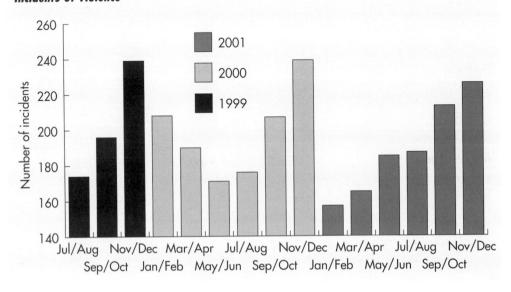

Incidents of disorder

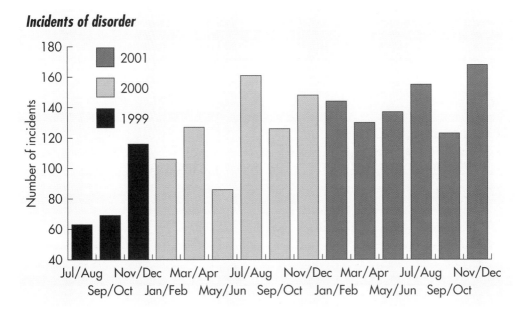

Table 4.1 *Percentage changes in 12-month totals of (a) violent incidents and (b) incidents of disorder, in TASC area, pre-and post project launch, according to different data sources*

	Percentage change over 12 months*	
	Disorder incidents	Violent incidents
Data source		
Incident data	+53%	+0.5%
Custody records	+68%	- 12%
Crime records	+57%	- 6%
All police data	+49%	- 2%
All A & E cases	N/A	+16%
A & E cases not known to police	N/A	-16%
Whole TASC database	+49%	- 4%

*Total for period July 2000 to June 2001, compared with total for period July 1999 to June 2000.

It is also worth noting that, during the last six months of the evaluation period (July to December 2001), the increase in disorderly incidents appeared to have slowed considerably: the total was only three per cent higher than that in July to December 2000. The equivalent figure for violent incidents was a rise of one per cent (see Appendix Table B.1).

Inside premises and on the street

A further interesting feature of incidents in the target sectors was a difference in trends between those occurring inside licensed premises and those occurring on the street. As Table 4.2 shows, the numbers of incidents occurring on the streets (both outside named pubs or clubs, and elsewhere on the streets) rose considerably more than those occurring inside licensed premises. This was the case despite the establishment of several large new clubs during the period concerned. The figures may be a reflection of, on the one hand, improved security and management *within* licensed premises – one of the key aims of the TASC project – but, on the other, of increased numbers of people on the streets late at night without any major changes in broader control strategies. As noted above, too, the main change on the streets was in levels of *disorder*, rather than violence.

Table 4.2   **Changes in numbers of incidents occurring inside and outside licensed premises, pre-project year to first year of project.**

| Period | Location of incident | | | | | |
	Inside lic. premises	Outside lic. premises	Elsewhere in street	In other premises	Not known	Total
July 1999 to June 2000	522	330	612	144	137	1,745
July 1999 to June 2000	580	452	726	130	87	1,975
% change	+11%	+37%	+19%	-10%	-36%	+13%

St Marys Street

A final important aspect of the overall picture is that the rise in violence and disorder was by no means uniform across the target sectors. Indeed, one particular street – St Marys Street, which is generally thought of as the main street in central Cardiff – accounts on its own for almost all the increase in the first year of the TASC project. The figures are as follows:

	July 1999 to June 2000	July 2000-to June 2001	Change
St Marys St	353	561	+59%
Other/not known	1,392	1,414	+2%
All	1,745	1,975	+13%

Where *violent* incidents were concerned, St Marys Street showed a rise of 42 per cent, compared with a fall elsewhere of 15 per cent. And for incidents of *disorder*, St Marys Street showed a rise of 99 per cent compared with a rise elsewhere of 38 per cent.

Moreover, the increases were seen in all locations in this area – incidents inside licensed premises here rose by 66 per cent, incidents outside named premises more than doubled (a rise of 151%), and incidents elsewhere in the street rose by 46 per cent.

It is almost certainly relevant that the southern end of this street has seen the greatest growth and concentration of new licensed premises over the past few years – to the extent that, as discussed earlier, the TASC team has argued that it is at its limit in terms of the capacity of the small space to cope with the numbers of drinkers, and have opposed new licences on these grounds.

Trends in injury

So far, then, it appears that the overall pattern of change during the TASC project was a significant rise in incidents of *disorder* soon after it was launched, but a relatively unchanged pattern of *violent* incidents, largely following the previous year's seasonal pattern. However, another way of looking at trends in violence is through the *numbers of people injured*, and particularly those seriously injured, in assaults.

Table 4.3 shows the numbers of people known to have been injured in alcohol-related assaults for each six-month period from July 1999 to December 2001 (note that the number of incidents is irrelevant here, as several people may be injured in one incident). The table, which combines data from police and hospital sources, also shows the numbers of people with injuries judged to be serious (principally, broken bones, broken or lost teeth, cuts requiring stitches, severe blows to the head).

Table 4.3   **Numbers of people injured, and seriously injured, in alcohol-related assaults, Cardiff city centre, July 1999 to December 2001**

	1999		2000		2001		1999-2000		2000-2001	
							Percentage increase			
	Level of injury		Level of injury		Level of injury		Level of injury			
	Any	Serious	Any	Serious	Any	Serious	Any	(Ser)	Any	(Ser)
Jan–June			299	73	419	163			40%	(126%)
Jul–Dec	410	93	496	159	525	188	21%	(71%)	6%	(18%)

It can be seen that, although (as discussed earlier) the numbers of violent incidents did not increase over the period, there appear to have been significant increases in the numbers of people injured, and especially in those injured *severely*. In fact, the latter almost doubled between the pre-project period and the first 12 months of its implementation. There may be some effect here, again, from the improvement in data collection at the hospital and the work of the project nurse. However, police records show a 27 per cent increase in incidents involving 'wounding or other acts endangering life' between the pre-project 12 months and the first 12 months after the project launch. They also indicate a considerable increase in larger-scale violent incidents involving three or more people, which were more likely to produce injuries to more than one person. In short, the 'injured persons per violent incident' rate increased from 0.6 to 0.8 from the pre-project to the project year, and the 'seriously injured persons per violent incident' rate doubled from 0.14 to 0.29.

It is difficult to explain this general rise in injuries, except by the general increase in drinking population in the city centre. The rise, in fact, is in stark contrast to the important finding that will be presented later in this chapter, that there were major *reductions* in injuries (and serious injuries) in the specific locations where there were sustained targeted police operations.

Comparisons with elsewhere

It is important to obtain some indication of whether the trends found in police sectors 29 and 30 are similar or different to those in other areas of South Wales. Of course, there is no equivalent of the TASC database elsewhere with which to compare trends in 'alcohol-related' violence and disorder. However, some comparisons can be made in terms of incidents of somewhat broader categories of violence and disorder recorded by the police. Table 4.4 compares trends in incidents of 'violence against the person' in these sectors with trends in the rest of the South Wales police force area: in both cases, the 'pre-project' period (July 1999 to June 2000) is compared with the first year of the project (July 2000 to June 2001). The types of incident included under 'violence against the person' are those where the report indicates that at least one physical (but not sexual) assault has occurred – that is, incidents classified as serious wounding, other wounding, common assault or 'other'. The two main differences between these records and those entered into the TASC database are that they include assaults not related to alcohol and domestic violence. For this reason, they should not be taken as conclusive evidence of trends in alcohol-related assaults in licensed premises or the streets, but as broad indicators.

Table 4.4 **Trends in police-recorded incidents of violence against the person, police sectors 29 & 30 and the remainder of the South Wales police force area**

	Percentage change in incidents	
	Sectors 29 & 30	Rest of force
Periods compared		
July–Sept 1999 and July–Sept 2000	-7%	-5%
Oct–Dec 1999 and Oct–Dec 1999	-16%	-9%
Jan–Mar 2000 and Jan–Mar 2000	-7%	+4%
Apr–June 2000 and Apr–June 2000	No change	+19%
July 1999–June 2000 and July 2000–June 2001	-8%	+2%

As can be seen, in each three-month period for the first year of the project, the targeted sectors in Cardiff showed a greater reduction in violence against the person, in comparison with the equivalent period of the previous year, than the rest of the force (in two periods, indeed, the figures rose elsewhere, but fell or stayed the same in the two sectors). Over the whole year, while incidents of violence against the person increased across the rest of South Wales by two per cent, they fell in the targeted sectors by eight per cent.

Where disorder is concerned, by contrast, the position is reversed. In the two targeted sectors, data from the police command and control system show a year-on-year increase of

11 per cent in incidents of disorder in licensed premises or in public places, compared to a mere one per cent increase in such incidents across the rest of the police force area. Again (with the proviso that the above figures include incidents which were not alcohol-related), this supports the general conclusion that if the TASC project had any impact, it was to help reduce the numbers of violent incidents, rather than to help reduce disorder.

Finally, it is worth briefly considering the possibility of 'displacement' – i.e. that increased police activity in the centre of Cardiff persuaded people prone to violent or disorderly behaviour to drink (and to cause trouble) elsewhere in the city or, indeed, in other South Wales towns. However, this is considered implausible, first of all because there are so many pubs and clubs in the city centre that even if people bent on 'causing trouble' noticed extra security in some of them they could easily move to another in the same area where there was less security; and secondly, because the evidence from the TASC database was that most of those involved as offenders had no previous convictions for violent behaviour and that most of the 'trouble' was spontaneous and unplanned. Unfortunately, owing to changes in divisional boundaries in April 2000, it is not possible to support or contradict this argument by comparing police incident figures for the target sectors with those for the rest of Cardiff.

Changes in licensed premises capacity

The main changes in the target sectors noted above – a decrease in violent incidents but a rise in disorderly incidents, and a decrease in incidents occurring inside pubs and clubs but an increase in incidents occurring in the streets – should be considered in the light of the other major changes referred to earlier – the rapid development of central Cardiff and the Bay as an entertainment centre, with major increases in visitor numbers and in the number and the total customer capacity of its pubs and clubs. During the pre-project year, July 1999 to June 2000, there was an average licensed premise capacity in the two sectors of about 45,000. During the first year of the project, the average capacity was around 49,600 – an increase of over 10 per cent. Of course, it cannot simply be assumed that one would expect an accompanying 10 per cent increase in violence and disorder. Nevertheless, one would certainly expect some increase: the example of St Marys Street indicates, at least, that the concentrated growth of new licensed premises in one small area is likely to bring with it an increase in alcohol-related disorder.

Conclusion: extent of crime reduction achieved

As in any 'before and after' study where there is no clear comparison area, it is difficult to state with any confidence what would have happened in the area had it not been for the implementation of the project. However, the various strands of evidence presented above suggest that some degree of crime reduction was achieved in the target sectors. First of all, the total number of known violent incidents fell by four per cent during the first 12 months of the implementation. Moreover, this occurred despite an increase in violent incidents elsewhere in South Wales; it also occurred despite a 10 per cent rise in licensed premise capacity in the area. Based on the above, it seems reasonable to assume that, without the project, the number of violent incidents in sectors 29 and 30 would have been at least as high in the first year of the project as in the pre-project year. It can thus be argued that the number of violent incidents prevented in this first year was at minimum 49 (i.e. the number by which the overall total fell compared to the previous year – see Appendix Table B.). Beyond this, it can be reasonably claimed that a combination of the 10 per cent increase in licensed premise capacity, plus the overall two per cent rise in recorded incidents of violence across South Wales, could have been expected to generate an *increase* in violent incidents in the target sectors. If (arbitrarily, but quite conservatively) this expected increase is placed at four per cent, it can be calculated that *the total number of violent incidents prevented by TASC during this year was around 100, equating to a reduction in such incidents of eight per cent*.[14] This is considered 'best estimate', and its 'cost-effectiveness' implications will be explored in the next chapter.

The above conclusion has, however, to be qualified in two important respects. First, although the numbers of violent incidents appear to have been reduced, there were many more *serious assaults* involved in such incidents than in the previous year – to the extent that it is difficult to make strong claims about TASC having prevented many (if any) serious injuries. And secondly, there was a considerable increase in incidents of *disorder* in the targeted area – a greater increase, indeed, than elsewhere in South Wales. It is thus difficult to claim from the overall figures that TASC prevented any 'disorder'.

Changes at 'hot spots'

As outlined in chapter 2, the TASC team identified from its database a number of individual licensed premises, as well as particular streets, with unusually high levels of violence or disorder. In some cases, the TASC sergeant visited and advised (or if necessary, warned) the manager of the premises in question, often focusing on the training and behaviour of security staff and/or bar staff. In a few cases, sizeable police operations were put in place. The focus here is on two main operations already described, Operations Alpha and Gamma, examining trends in incidents in the particular locations targeted in relation to the dates of the operations.

14 With an increase of four per cent, the 1,178 known violent incidents occurring between July 1999 and June 2000 would have grown to 1,225 in the next 12 months. The actual total known over the latter period was 1,129 (Appendix Table B.), i.e. 96 fewer than 'expected'.

Operation Alpha

Figure 4.2 shows in graph form all known incidents occurring inside, or just outside, the two large dance clubs (Alpha and Beta) which were the subject of Operation Alpha. As noted earlier, this operation was focused mainly on Club Alpha, and entailed a package of measures including regular inspections of facilities, close dialogue with managers, greatly increased plain-clothes and uniformed presence, close examination of door staff licences, and liaison with local taxi services for efficient dispersal of customers. It lasted for an eight week period from mid July to mid September 2000, shortly after the official launch of the TASC project. This period, it will be remembered, saw both disorder rates and injuries accelerating rapidly across the two police sectors as a whole.

Figure 4.2   Trends in violence and disorder, two licensed premises targeted by significant police operations in late summer 2000

Club Alpha

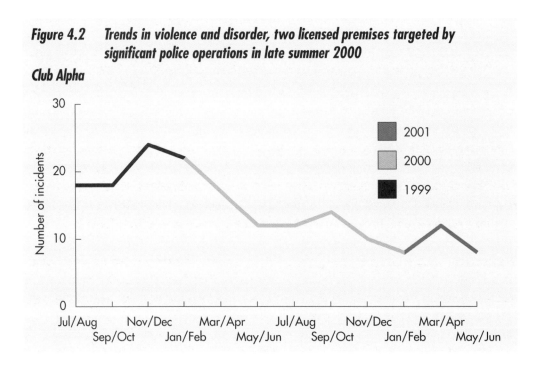

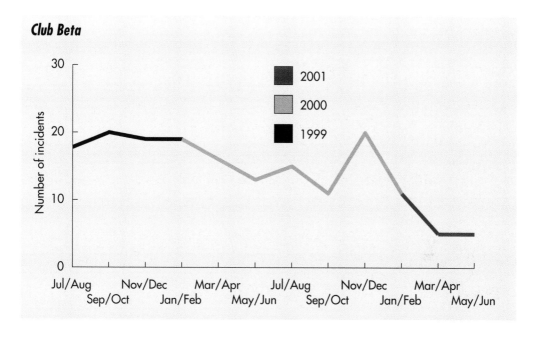

Club Beta

As the graphs clearly show, both locations not only 'bucked the trend' in the short term, but sustained lower rates of violence and disorder for the ensuing 12 months. Club Alpha saw a total of 111 incidents in the year July 1999 to June 2000 reduced to 66 incidents in the following 12 months. Club Beta saw an equivalent reduction from 105 to 67. These figures represent falls of 41 per cent and 36 per cent, respectively – comparing very favourably with the overall *increase* in the area of 13 per cent (as shown in Appendix Table B).

In this context, it is worth mentioning a third club that was heavily targeted by TASC, albeit on a lesser scale. This took place mainly in November and December 2000, and involved frequent meetings between the TASC sergeant and the management and staff of the club. This was a new club, which had opened in the summer and had 'got off to a bad start' in terms of violence and disorder. While the figures are quite small, once again there is evidence of a sustained downward trend beginning after a strongly focused set of interventions. In the first six months of the club's existence, from July to December 2000, there were 44 incidents known at this location. Over the next six months there were 37, and in July to December 2001, only 26.

Similar findings apply to all three locations in terms of injuries recorded (either in police or hospital records). In the case of Alpha and Beta, the annual totals of injuries pre- and post intervention fell from 67 to 35 and from 59 to 40; in the case of the new club, the three successive six-monthly totals of injuries were 31, 26, and 17. Indeed, on all related variables tested, such as attendance at hospital, and number of seriously injured people, the trend in these locations appears to be in the opposite direction to that in the sector as a whole. This suggests that, while the TASC project may not have succeeded in reducing the numbers of serious injuries in assaults across the area as a whole, it did so in relation to particular premises that it targeted as high risk.

Operation Gamma

In contrast to the above successes in and around heavily targeted individual premises, the operation which was conducted in relation to two particular streets (Operation 'Gamma' – see Chapter 2 above) does not appear to have had the same kind of impact. It will be recalled that the streets in question (which are some distance apart) each contain several pubs and clubs in close proximity, and were identified as clear 'hot spots'. The operation was conducted over eight weeks from January to March 2001, and entailed a high visibility police presence as well as some work with clubs and pubs in the two streets.

During the months of the operation and for a few months afterwards, incidents of violence and disorder in these two streets remained at a slightly lower level than in the equivalent period of the previous year (see Figure 4.3). However, in the second half of the year (from September onwards), the numbers of incidents climbed steeply.

Conclusions

Although not too much should be 'read' from a few examples, the evidence from the operations described suggests that, while targeting individual clubs (and in particular their management practices and the behaviour and training of their door staff) may have a considerable and *lasting* effect, operations targeted at whole streets may have, if anything, only a temporary effect.

In terms of the outcome evaluation, it can be argued that the project can plausibly be credited with preventing at least 83 incidents in the two clubs during the year after the operations (i.e. the reduction in incidents compared with the previous year.) Assuming 30 per cent of these to involve disorder, an estimated minimum of 28 'disorderly incidents' prevented by TASC, can be added to the estimates of prevented violent incidents given above (of course, it would be 'double counting' to include the violent incidents prevented, as these already form part of the overall figures for the sectors).

Figure 4.3 **Trends in incidents 2000 to 2001, two streets targeted in Operation Gamma, January to March 2001**

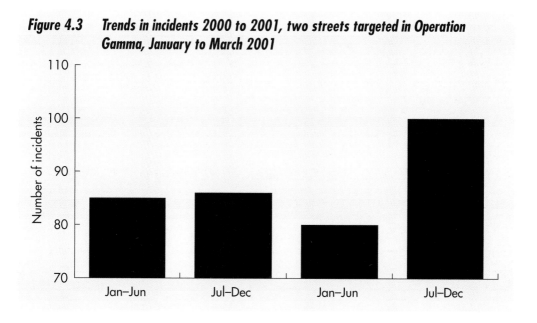

Summary

Over the 18-month evaluation period when the TASC project was in operation, there was a decrease in the numbers of violent incidents known to have occurred in the targeted area. The first year of full implementation saw a fall of four per cent and the next six months saw little change. This reduction took place despite a significant rise in licensed premise capacity in the area, and despite increases in recorded incidents of violence against the person elsewhere in South Wales. The best estimate is that in its first year of operation, the impact of TASC was to reduce the expected level of violent incidents by eight per cent (i.e. by about 100 incidents).

By contrast, the project appeared to have little effect on incidents of *disorder*, which rose during the first year by 49 per cent. However (unlike violent incidents), the great majority of these occurred on the streets, rather than inside pubs and clubs, and it was here that the bulk of the increase was apparent. Moreover, nearly all the rise was accounted for by one street in Cardiff, which contained the densest concentration of pubs and clubs and where a number of new premises opened over a short period.

In contrast to the overall trend, there is evidence of substantial reductions in incidents (of all kinds) in and outside clubs where well organised targeted policing operations were conducted (in two cases these lasted for eight weeks and involved packages of measures including increased uniformed police presence, work with management, and door staff training and reforms). These reductions were sustained, and it is estimated that at least 83 incidents (28 of them 'disorder') were prevented over 12 months. An operation targeted on two streets also saw reductions, but these were not sustained.

5.   Costs and cost effectiveness

Context

This chapter considers the cost-effectiveness of the TASC project. Firstly by presenting the key results of the cost evaluation with particular focus on the distribution of the costs incurred (Appendix C provides brief further details about the cost estimation process). Next focusing on the cost-effectiveness of TASC in relation to the cost of the alternative – 'what would have happened if TASC had not been implemented.' To do this the authors first link evidence of the effectiveness of the TASC project to monetary valuation of crimes prevented. They then compare this valuation with the cost of the TASC project in order to determine cost-effectiveness. Finally they offer evidence of 'value-for-money' provided by Operation Alpha, the most effective targeted policing intervention.

Results

TASC costs

The total economic cost of the TASC interventions described in Chapter 2 was estimated to be £488,000. Around £335,000 worth of resources were consumed in the set-up period and first year after the launch of the project (the period used in the calculations of effectiveness) and of these, about a third represented general set-up costs. More broadly, the distribution of these costs can be considered across interventions, time and through the cost burden placed on partner organisations. A full breakdown is shown in Appendix Table 3.1.

In terms of the interventions, the 'Support Nurse' initiative was most expensive (incurring costs of around £85,000),[15] followed by 'Door Staff Training' (£66,000) and 'Media Campaign' (£54,000). The targeted policing intervention costs were about £40,000, of which 'Operation Alpha' contributed just over half. The least costly intervention (at around £32,000) was the additional activity associated with the re-modelled 'Door Staff Registration Scheme.'

It should be noted that the central support function – encompassing the project manager, training sergeant, data analyst, administrator and associated costs, together with the

---

15 As noted in Chapter 2, in the light of experience, it was generally agreed that it was not necessary to employ a nurse of this seniority to perform the tasks required. Clearly, if a more junior person were to be used, the costs of a replication of the project would be somewhat lower than those analysed in this chapter.

opportunity costs of steering group members and other 'levered-in' personnel – impacted substantially on overall TASC costs, contributing around 60 per cent of the total figure. In terms of replicating the project elsewhere, however, general set-up costs would be more appropriately apportioned over a longer time span than offered by the pilot project. This would suggest a falling average cost for intervention activity, and by approximating ongoing costs as variable costs our could expect annual ongoing costs to be around £200,000 for the roll-out of the TASC project at year 2000 prices.

Nevertheless, analysis of costs over time revealed that about 25 per cent of costs were incurred in setting-up TASC interventions and while most (87%) were incurred in the general set-up period (before July 2000) the overall stream of TASC project costs did not readily approximate to the broadly anticipated pattern of high levels of early expenditure followed by falling costs over time. Readers should however be aware that the 'COV-AID' and 'Servewise' interventions were implemented late in the project and had little impact on the resulting crime outcomes. Ignoring the costs of these interventions, overall project costs fall to just under £400,000 and the expected cost stream pattern becomes more observable.

The distribution of costs on various partner organisations was considered by identifying the degree to which these organisations provided resources 'freely' or 'in-kind'. Around 28 per cent of project costs were identified as being of this type, with the door staff training scheme (50% of total cost) and Licensees Forum (40% of total cost) utilising 'in-kind' resources most intensively.[16] Less than £20,000 (6%) of the central support costs represented levered-in input and this came mainly from the time supplied by local steering group members.

Cost-effectiveness

In Chapter 4 it was (conservatively) estimated that during TASC's first year of full implementation, the number of expected violent incidents in the target area fell by around 100. On this basis, comparison with the full costs for first-year implementation reveals an estimated cost of £3,200 per assault prevented.[17] Alternatively, if set-up costs are excluded and the calculation is based only on annual implementation (variable) costs, the cost per assault prevented emerges as about £2,000.

---

16 Reflecting the opportunity cost of door staff attending the training and licensed premises managers attending forum meetings.

17 As noted above, set-up and first year costs came to around £330,000. Two interventions – 'COV-AID' and 'Servewise' – were not relevant for comparison with the outcomes discussed in Chapter 4. Excluding the set-up and first year costs incurred in these interventions, total relevant costs equalled about £320,000.

As 'other wounding' (i.e. principally s47 offences of 'assault occasioning actual bodily harm') was by far the most common category of offence associated with violent incidents in the sectors concerned (accounting for about 70% of those recorded by the police), the simplest approach to financial calculations about prevented assaults is to use this as the crime type. The Home Office economists Brand and Price (2000) have estimated a saving to society of £2,040 per prevented incident of 'other wounding'.[18] This represents an estimate of the average total costs incurred by society in response, as a consequence, and in anticipation of, this type of crime. Hence, by comparing prevented incidents with this monetary value it can be estimated that without the TASC project, the cost of the additional crime to society would have been £204,000.

On the above assumptions, a like-for-like comparison of TASC project costs for the period July 2000 to June 2001 produces an estimated net dissaving (cost) to society of £116,000.[19] However, if compared to the estimated annual implementation costs of £200,000 the net dissaving disappears and a net saving of £4,000 is indicated.

It is of course likely that not all prevented assaults are best represented by 'other woundings', but that some would have entailed only 'common assault' and (probably) some would have been serious woundings (in essence, offences inflicting 'grievous bodily harm' and chargeable under s18 or s20). Police statistics for the two sectors in 1999 to 2000 indicate that about 15 per cent of crimed incidents of assault in the two police sectors involved common assault and 15 per cent serious woundings. Indeed, as shown in Chapter 3, over a quarter of all known violent incidents resulted in deep cuts or broken bones, and could therefore have potentially attracted a charge of wounding. Brand and Price (1999) place the hugely differing values of £550 and £130,000 per incident, respectively, for common assault and serious wounding, so it is clear that to use either or both of these categories in the calculations, as opposed to 'other wounding' alone, would make a major difference to the conclusions. Indeed, were just *one* of the incidents prevented to involve a serious wounding, then the TASC project would emerge as the 'value for money' option even when full set-up costs are included. And if several such assaults were prevented, the savings would be very substantial. (Conversely, substitution of common assault for some of the 'other wounding' cases would reduce the value of TASC, but by a relatively small degree).

In other words, if, following the above police statistics, 15 of the 100 prevented assaults were assumed to involve serious wounding and 15 common assault, *the overall 'net saving to society' would be nearly £2 million*. However, as pointed out in Chapter 4, there was a considerable increase during the evaluation period in the proportion of violent incidents

18 This includes an adjustment by the authors to their figure to 2000 prices.
19 i.e. £320,000 minus £204,000.

which involved serious injury, and it cannot therefore be assumed with any confidence that TASC prevented many (if any) assaults of this kind.[20]

Finally, no inclusion has been made in the above calculations for incidents of disorder. Average monetary values or costs for such incidents are less readily available, but they were mainly low level incidents involving individuals rather than large groups, so it may be assumed that the costs were relatively small. As shown in Chapter 4, there was an overall increase in disorder in the two police sectors and, although it was calculated that around 30 such incidents may have been prevented in one particular location, by Operation Alpha, it cannot safely be assumed that the project achieved a net reduction of expected incidents of disorder across the targeted area as a whole.

Conclusions

Cost-effectiveness evaluation allows comparison on a 'value for money' basis of interventions competing for scarce resources. The decision rule is to choose the option with the least cost per unit outcome. However, with no immediate project comparator the results of the TASC project can only be compared with the cost of the alternative – that is, what would have happened had TASC not been implemented. In making this comparison, the cost of the TASC project was compared with the estimated number of prevented assaults (100).

The resulting measure of cost-effectiveness was calculated at £3,200 per offence prevented if TASC set-up costs are included, or £2,000 per offence on the basis of annual implementation costs alone. Whether these costs are higher or lower than the net cost to society of each incident prevented depends largely on assumptions about the specific types of assault which were prevented. Very different monetary values are assigned to 'serious wounding', 'other wounding' and 'common assault' (£130,000, £2,040 and £550, respectively). If it is simply assumed that all 100 offences prevented were 'other woundings', the TASC project emerges as either roughly 'breaking even' or with a small 'net loss to society', depending on whether set-up costs are included in the calculation. However, if it is assumed that just two incidents among the 100 prevented would have involved more serious violence, the project emerges as strong 'value for money'.

In this respect – and with the strong evidence for the cost-effectiveness of Operation Alpha – the evaluation of the cost-effectiveness of the TASC project supports the conclusions drawn in Chapter 4.

---

20 This point is further emphasised in the analysis of the targeted policing operations and in particular Operation Alpha. Here estimated prevented costs for first year falls in violent crime (again valued as 'other wounding') reveal a net benefit of around £90,000, but again this figure could fluctuate markedly according to the exact 'type' of crime.

6.   Summary and conclusions

The TASC project was launched in July 2000 and was evaluated over a period of 18 months. Its main aims were to reduce alcohol-related crime and disorder in two police sectors covering central Cardiff and Cardiff Bay. Its main interventions were:

- focused dialogue between the police and members of the licensed trade;
- measures aimed at improving the quality and behaviour of door staff;
- attempts to influence licensing policy and practice;
- measures aimed at publicising the problem of alcohol-related violent crime;
- targeted policing operations directed at crime and disorder 'hot spots';
- a cognitive behavioural programme for repeat offenders ('COV-AID');
- a training programme for bar staff ('Servewise');
- a programme of education about alcohol for school age children; and
- support for victims of alcohol-related assaults attending hospital.

An essential 'tool' used by TASC throughout its operation was a dedicated database, maintained by the data analyst, which combined and correlated data from a range of police sources and the Accident and Emergency Unit of the main Cardiff hospital. A key vehicle for its activities was through the Licensees Forum, set up with encouragement from the project, which provided a channel for communication and co-operation with virtually all managers of licensed premises in the target area.

An examination of patterns of violence in the city centre revealed that:

- Alcohol related incidents were very heavily concentrated in time, with Friday and Saturday nights between them accounting for nearly half of all incidents.
- Sixty-one per cent of all known incidents involved physical violence, the remainder being incidents of 'disorder'.
- Over half of all incidents were linked to individual licensed premises, occurring either inside them or in the street directly outside them.
- Violent incidents were most common in or around specific licensed premises, while incidents of disorder were more likely to occur elsewhere on the streets.
- Most incidents involved only one or two people.
- Most of those involved as offenders or victims were young white males.

- Forty-two per cent of those arrested had previous arrests for violent or public order offences.
- 'Door staff' were involved as victims or alleged assailants in 16 per cent of all incidents involving violence, and in 34 per cent of all such incidents taking place inside pubs or clubs.
- Sixty-one door staff were arrested over the 30-month period examined.
- The most common form of assault was punching or kicking, but at least 10 per cent of cases involved bottles or glasses; the use of knives was rare.
- Most injuries were fairly minor cuts and bruises to the face or head, but 15 per cent of victims of assault suffered broken bones and 12 per cent major cuts requiring stitches. Thirty per cent of assaults were classified as 'serious'.

Outcomes

A comparison of the first 12 months after the launch of the project (July 2000 to June 2001) with the previous 12 months indicated that there was an *overall decrease of four per cent in incidents involving alcohol-related assaults.* By contrast, over the same period there was a *49 per cent increase in incidents of alcohol-related disorder.*

The fall in alcohol-related assaults (which was reflected in a variety of police record sources and in the records of A & E cases which were not known to the police) is highly encouraging for the TASC project, especially during a period when the numbers of incidents of violence against the person were rising elsewhere in South Wales and when there was a more than ten per cent increase in licensed premise capacity and the numbers of people drinking late at night in central Cardiff.

It is of course impossible to say with certainty how many assaults would have occurred had TASC not been in existence, but taking into account the background changes mentioned above, the researchers' best estimate is that, overall, *during its first year of full implementation, the project helped to reduce the expected level of violent incidents by eight per cent – or by about 100 incidents.*

The above results can be translated into cost-effectiveness terms. If the 100 offences prevented are assumed to have been cases of 'other wounding' (i.e. medium serious offences that would be prosecuted under s47 of the Offences Against the Person Act – widely referred to as 'assault occasioning actual bodily harm'), the cost per offence prevented emerges as £3,200 – more than the estimated average cost of an offence of this kind. On this assumption, then, TASC does not appear to offer value for money when compared to the alternative – 'what would have happened had TASC not been implemented'. However if any *one* of the 100 assaults prevented would have been of a more serious nature (i.e. s18 or s20 woundings, costed at £130,000 per offence), then TASC offers the most cost-effective option. While caution must be shown in this area, it is likely that at least a few of the offences prevented would have been serious, and hence the 'cost-effectiveness' results support the positive conclusions about the effectiveness of TASC drawn in Chapter 4. The research also provides some cost-effectiveness evidence for the value of the targeted policing operations.

By contrast, where disorder is concerned the results were disappointing. However, it must be remembered that 'alcohol-related disorder' is a much more slippery concept than 'alcohol-related assault', and that the figures given are more susceptible to changes in police activities and recording practices (there were also, unlike assaults, no figures from A & E to support or contradict them). It is possible that the increased attention to disorder created by the setting up of TASC resulted in police officers being readier to use the Public Order Act to deal with some incidents that they would earlier have defused with warnings and perhaps not recorded. Moreover, even if the figures are accepted at face value, two other important points should be noted:

1. The increase in disorder slowed considerably after the first few months of TASC 'going live': the increases for the first three six-month periods after launch, in relation to the equivalent period of the previous year, were 75 per cent, 29 per cent and three per cent respectively.

2. Virtually all the rise in disorder was accounted for by one street in Cardiff – the street with the densest concentration of pubs and clubs and where a number of new premises opened over a short period.

Perhaps the most promising and clear-cut findings related to reductions in violent and disorderly incidents occurring in or just outside individual pubs and clubs which were the subject of carefully targeted policing operations. The most successful of these, lasting eight weeks, was followed by reductions of 41 per cent and 36 per cent in such incidents in and around the two clubs targeted. The reductions were sustained over time, and it is calculated that at least 83 incidents (28 of them 'disorder') were prevented. On the other hand, operations targeted at two separate streets, rather than individual premises, appeared to be successful only in the short term, with early reductions not being sustained.

Overall, the TASC project appears to have been most successful in terms of its targeted work with individual premises. Its most fruitful partnership arrangements were with the Licensees Forum, where a co-operative dialogue was set up with local pub and club managers, and through which joint attempts were made to improve security arrangements – including staff training – in individual premises where the TASC database indicated that the numbers of violent or disorderly incidents were high or rising.

On the other hand, at least during the evaluation period, it had more problems in its attempts to persuade 'key players ' in the County Council, breweries or other relevant companies to adopt broader strategic approaches to the prevention of late night alcohol-related violence and disorder. Probably its greatest successes in this respect concerned the establishment of better registration, training and disciplinary systems for door staff, but even here it came up against considerable resistance and delay. It made little headway in influencing planning policy or stopping further growth of licensed premises in particular locations it considered 'saturated'. It eventually brokered a scheme for late night buses, but had little success in relation to taxi firms. And despite persuading one major company to discontinue a problematic 'happy hour', it failed to get general agreement to changes in alcohol marketing strategies.

Lessons in 'good practice'

A number of examples of good practice were identified. These include:

- A project manager at a sufficient level of seniority, and a well resourced project team, including a data analyst with detailed knowledge of police data systems such as Command and Control and CIS.
- The full integration of the project into police objectives and priorities, including representation at Tasking and Co-ordinating Groups.
- The creation of effective links with managers of licensed premises, especially through an active Licensees Forum.
- The maintenance of an accurate and up-to-date dedicated database, using both police and hospital data sources.
- The use of the database not only to identify problems as they emerge, but to guide remedial visits to licensed premises by licensing officers, as 'concrete evidence' with which to persuade managers to take action and, in extreme cases, as evidence to oppose licences or object to specific practices such as 'drinks promotion' schemes.

- The development of an effective, proactive training programme for door staff.
- The development of greater regulation of door staff.
- The deployment of a member of the project team (in this case the training sergeant) on the disciplinary committee for door staff.
- Wide promotion of the project's objectives using a range of innovative sources eg bus campaigns, websites, electronic public information display screens.
- The appointment of a project nurse based in the hospital, to support victims, encourage more reporting of assaults, and assist the production of more comprehensive data.
- Attempts to engage major players in both the public and private sectors in broader dialogue about the strategic management of the 'late night economy' in the city centre.

Appendix A   Map

Example of GIS mapping of incidents in central Cardiff, covering one month [21]

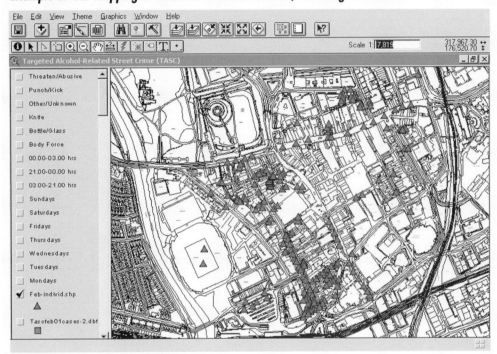

21 This map was kindly produced for the research team by Paul Pan of the Crime Reduction Unit, National
    Assembly for Wales.

Appendix B

Additional tables and figures

Table B **(a) All known incidents of alcohol-related disorder, Cardiff city centre, July 1999 to Dec 2001**

	1999	2000	2001	Annual change	
	Pre-project	Pre-project	Project	99–00	00–01
Jan–Feb		106	144		+36%
Mar–Apr		127	130		+2%
May–Jun		86	137		+59%
Six-month total		319	411		+29%
	Pre-project	Project	Project		
Jul–Aug	63	161	155	+156%	+1%
Sept–Oct	69	126	123	+83%	–
Nov–Dec	116	148	168	+28%	+2%
Six-month total	248	435	446	+75%	+3%

(b) All known incidents of alcohol-related violence, Cardiff city centre, July 1999 to Dec 2001

	1999	2000	2001	Annual change	
	Pre-project	Pre-project	Project	99–00	00–01
Jan–Feb		208	157		25%
Mar–Apr		190	165		13%
May–Jun		171	185		+8%
Six-month total		569	507		-11%
	Pre-project	Project	Project		
Jul–Aug	174	176	187	+1%	+6%
Sept–Oct	196	207	213	+6%	+3%
Nov–Dec	239	239	226	–	-5%
Six-month total	609	622	626	+2%	+1%

Figure B   **Trends in all incidents of violence and disorder appearing in police records (incident, crime and custody records combined), July 1999 to June 2001**

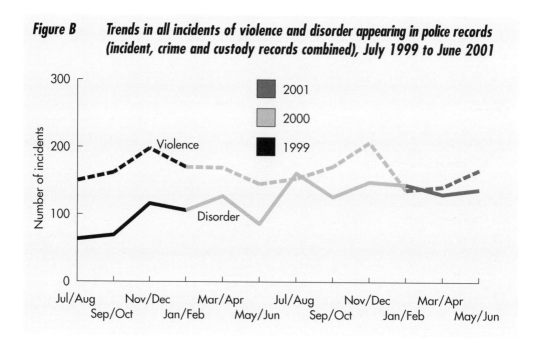

Trends in numbers of incidents involving recorded offences of violence and disorder, July 1999 to June 2001

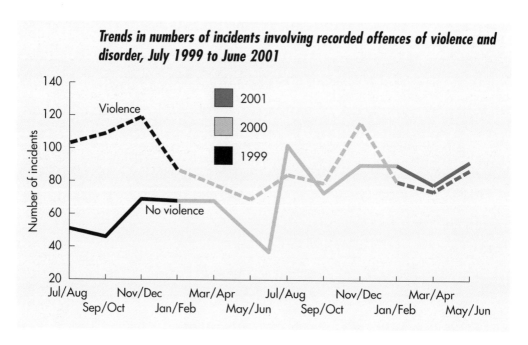

Appendix C   Additional data on cost effectiveness

Estimating the costs

The research required a comprehensive approach to costing. This involved collecting costs for each intervention in relation to:

- direct staff salaries plus on-costs;
- indirect staff such as support function (supervision, clerical etc.), senior management, contribution to central personnel and finance;
- direct overheads such as TASC office costs – rent, stationery and so on – and travel;
- capital purchases; and
- human capital investment.

Project-related expenditure was tracked from financial data supplied by the police finance department. Information on resources supplied outside the Crime Reduction Programme funding – such as partner agency input, police line management and re-assigned capital equipment – was obtained through ongoing interviews with members of the TASC project manager and direct contact with relevant partner agency staff. The methodology emphasised the use of existing data sources – for example, police diary records, invoices and intervention specific reports – to identify, quantify and value input resources.

Appendix Table 3.1 shows a summary picture of all the TASC costs, broken down by type of intervention, set-up costs, grant-funded and levered-in costs, and showing both primary and supplemental outputs.

Table 3.1:   TASC Costs

Intervention	Set-up Cost (£)	Total Cost (£) CRP funded (£)	Total Cost (£) Levered-in (£)	Primary Output Measure	Primary Output Cost per unit output (£)	Supplemental Outputs Measure	Supplemental Outputs Cost per unit output (£)
Targeting premises	11,585	29,796	10,307	Average cost per campaign	13,368	Average cost per premises covered	8,021
Media campaign	13,102	47,285	6,333	Average weekly cost of publicity campaigns	516	Average weekly cost of campaigns	1671
						Average cost per person viewing bus campaign	0.05
Schools initiative	11,067	28,930	9,813	Average cost per presentation to young people	1761	Cost per young person receiving presentations	35
Licensed premises staff	10,240	28,328	11,757	Cost per bar staff member completing "Serve-wise"	871		
COV-Aid	5,188	35,334	10,465	Cost per offender completing COV-Aid	15,266	Cost per offenders starting COV-Aid	9160
Licensees' Forum	15,515	28,557	18,745	Cost per forum meeting	3153		
Door staff training	11,252	32,692	33,489	Cost per door staff member trained	299	Cost per course run	5091
Licensee liaison	11,065	28,334	9,567	Cost per visit to licensed premises	190		
Door staff registration scheme	10,061	28,328	3,581	Average cost per disciplinary hearings	1595		
Support nurse	20,034	66,545	18,514	Number of people interviewed	113	Cost per referral made to victim support	378
Total	119,109	354,129	132,571				

References

Brand S. and Price R. (2000) *The Economic and Social Costs of Crime*, Home Office Research Study 217. London: Home Office.

Cardiff Research Centre (2000) *Cardiff Visitor Survey*. Cardiff: Cardiff County Council.

Deehan, A. (1999) *Alcohol and Crime: Taking Stock*. Policing and Reducing Crime Unit Research Series, Paper 3. London: Home Office.

Dhiri S. and Brand S. (1999) *Analysis of Costs and Benefits: Guidance for Eevaluators* (Crime Reduction Programme Guidance 1) London: Home Office.

Graham, K. and Homel, R. (1997) 'Creating Safer Bars' in M. Plant, E. Single and T. Stockwell (eds) *Alcohol: Minimising the Harm – What Works?* London: Free Association Press.

Hobbs, D, Hadfield, P., Lister, S. and Winlow, S. (2002) 'Door Lore': The Art and Economics of Intimidation. *British Journal of Criminology*, 42, 2: 352–370.

Hobbs, D., Lister, S., Hadfield, P., Winlow, S. and Hall, S. (2000). 'Receiving Shadows: Liminality, Governance and the Night-Time Economy' *British Journal of Sociology*, 51, 4:701–17.

Justices' Clerks' Society (1999) *Good Practice Guide: Licensing*. London: Justices' Clerks' Society.

LGA (2002) *All Day and all of the Night? An LGA Discussion Paper*. London: Local Government Association.

Light, R. (2000) 'Liberalising liquor licensing law: order into chaos?' *New Law Journal*, June 23: 926-9.

Lister, S. Hadfield, P., Hobbs, D. and Winlow, S. (2001) 'Accounting for bouncers: occupational licensing as a mechanism for regulation' *Criminal Justice* 1(4): 363–84.

Maguire, M., Morgan, R. and Nettleton, H. (2001) *Early Lessons from the Crime Reduction Programme: Tackling Alcohol Related Street Crime in Cardiff.* Home Office Briefing Note 9/01, London: Home Office.

Phillips, C. and Bowling, B. (2002) 'Racism, Ethnicity, Crime and Criminal Justice' in M. Maguire, R. Morgan and R. Reiner (eds) *The Oxford Handbook of Criminology* (Third edition) Oxford: Oxford University Press.

Purser, R. (1997) *Prevention Approaches to Alcohol Related Crime – A Review of a Community Based Initiative from a UK Midlands City.* Birmingham: Aquarius.

Shepherd, J., Shapland, M. and Scully, C. (1989) 'Recording of violent offences by the police: an accident and emergency department perspective' *Med Sci Law* 29:251–7.

Simmons, J. (2000) *Review of Crime Statistics: A Discussion Document.* London: Home Office.

Social Issues Research Centre (2002) *Counting the Cost: The Measurement and Recording of Alcohol-Related Violence and Disorder.* London: The Portman Group.

RDS Publications

Requests for Publications

Copies of our publications and a list of those currently available may be obtained from:

Home Office
Research, Development and Statistics Directorate
Communication Development Unit
Room 275, Home Office
50 Queen Anne's Gate
London SW1H 9AT
Telephone: 020 7273 2084 (answerphone outside of office hours)
Facsimile: 020 7222 0211
E-mail: publications.rds@homeoffice.gsi.gov.uk

alternatively

why not visit the RDS web-site at
        Internet: http://www.homeoffice.gov.uk/rds/index.htm

where many of our publications are available to be read on screen or downloaded for printing.